Three-Dimensional Analysis

Three-Dimensional Analysis

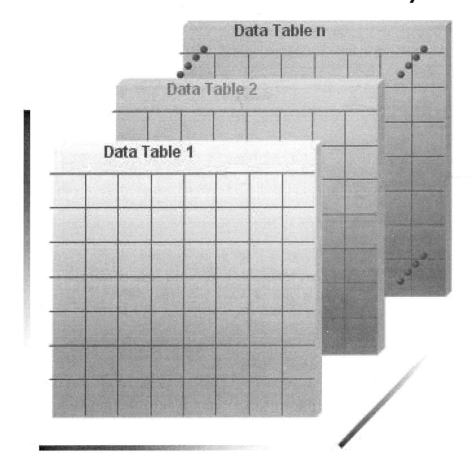

Data Profiling Techniques

By

Ed Lindsey

ISBN: 978-0-9800833-0-9

Contents

Preface

DATA profiling is the process of examining the content, structure, and quality of data in order to better understand it. The concept is a relatively new one. It was originally introduced to the market by Evoke in the late 1990s. Since then a number of vendors have introduced data profiling software.

However, none of the vendors has spent much time teaching data profiling techniques. They teach how to use using their software to profile data. They focus their efforts on what the software does; it's up to you to figure out how to use it to understand your data better.

This book will help you better understand your data. It will show you some techniques you can use to get the most information about your data using a profiling tool or some other method. A date field is a simple example. There are a number of techniques you can use to test for anomalies in a date field. These help you validate or invalidate the information contained in that field.

While the book is geared toward using a profiling tool to help you understand your data, many of the techniques included in the book do not explicitly require one.

Most of this book is focused on techniques to find anomalies in your data. I start with why you might want to profile your data. I give specific real world examples of issues I have found with different companies' data. I move on to explain what data profiling is and then where to start. Next, I discuss general data profiling techniques, providing more details on specific techniques for different industries. Finally, I describe specific data profiling techniques for special data fields, like a vehicle identification number (VIN) and Social Security numbers.

The book is based upon years of practical field experience profiling data for many companies. I use real world examples throughout the book. After reading this book, you will get a bigger benefit from the software your company spends hundreds of thousands of dollars on to accelerate your data-related projects or identify data quality issues.

Typical readers for this book include:

- Business User/Analyst – Any business user who wants to understand the underlying data quality better for their business unit's needs.
- Database Administrator (DBA) – Database administrators who need to explore the data and structure of the databases they administer.
- Extract, Transform, and Load (ETL) Developer – ETL developers who want to get clear specifications for their development needs.
- Profiling Facilitator / Project Manager – Members of the team that who been trained and are expected to run the profiling software or are running a data-related project that will include profiling the data.
- Data Steward – Like business users, data stewards also need to get a better understanding of the data and metadata for which they are responsible.
- Data Modeler – Modelers who want to understand and verify the structure of their systems or are in the process of creating new models. They can use the techniques to verify the data will fit their models.

Each of these different team members will benefit from reading this book and using the knowledge gained from it.

At the time this book was written, all information was believed to be accurate. However, data-related information continues to change. For example, a DEA number now includes additional valid letters. Phone area codes are being added. ZIP codes constantly change. Eventually, VIN numbers will have to change to accommodate more dates. As I explain in the book, use the information as guidelines, expecting that it will change over time.

All of the screen shots are copyrighted by and appear courtesy of Informatica Corporation. Informatica can be reached at:

Informatica Corporation Headquarters
100 Cardinal Way
Redwood City, CA 94063
Tel: (650) 385-5000
Toll-free US: (800) 653-3871
Fax: (650) 385-5500
www.informatica.com

I hope you enjoy this book and feel free to contact me with any questions or concerns.

Ed Lindsey

Ed_lindsey@hotmail.com

www.dataprofilingtechniques.com

Acknowledgements

I WOULD like to thank my wife Kathy for putting up with the long nights and weekends required to accomplish this endeavor. I would also like to thank Dave Reed for jokingly suggesting, "What are you going to do next, write a book?" I want to thank Nick Dobbins for painstakingly reading the book for content and quality. I want to thank Tommy Drummond for having the perseverance and stamina to push this project through. I also need to thank Tim Ogren, who explained to me that I could still have a beer and type at the same time. Lastly, I want to thank all my customers over the years for allowing me the opportunity to assist them in their quest for better data quality. Without all their issues, I would not have all the great examples referenced in this book.

Chapter 1

WHY PROFILE YOUR DATA?

What Industry Has to Say

IT'S a complete mess. They don't even know what they don't know.—Caroline Flint, being briefed on the situation by Connecting for Health (CfH) chief executive, Richard Granger

"Accurate data is a fundamental requirement of good information systems. And yet most information systems contain significant amounts of inaccurate data, and most enterprises lack enough of a basic understanding of the concepts of information quality to recognize or change the situation. Accurate data is an important dimension of information quality—the most important dimension."—Jack Olsen

"Information quality is not an esoteric notion; it directly affects the effectiveness and efficiency of business processes. Information quality also plays a major role in customer satisfaction."—Larry P. English

"Poor data quality is costly. It lowers customer satisfaction, adds expense, and makes it more difficult to run a business and pursue tactical improvements such as data warehouses and re-engineering."—Thomas C. Redman

"...three-quarters (of participating companies) reported significant problems as a result of defective data, with a third failing to bill or collect receivables as a result."—PricewaterhouseCoopers survey of 600 CIOs, IT directors, and similar executives

"CRM's potential to provide better customer service and in turn boost revenue has caught the attention of many companies.

But a number of CRM deployments are thwarted by faulty, inconsistent data sets that prevent enterprises from having a clear, unified profile of each customer."—Paul Krill

A Related Story: Data, the Dirty Dog

February 28, 2007: Gartner believes that 25 percent of critical data in Fortune 100 companies will continue to be flawed in the next two years.

By "flawed" Gartner means the information will be inaccurate, incomplete, or duplicated. They are calling it "dirty data," as Gartner calls it, and it is a problem that looks set to continue to affect three-quarters of large enterprises until 2010.

Gartner says dirty data leverages significant burdens and costs. Higher customer turnover could result while expenses in regular process such as mail-outs and missed sales opportunities could blowout from incorrect information. Overall, data quality has a significant impact on business initiatives, from sales to marketing and back-office functions such as budgeting, manufacturing, and distribution.

In the surveys of 2001 and 2005, TDWI asked, "Has your company suffered losses, problems, or costs due to poor quality data?" Respondents answering "yes" grew from 44 percent in 2001 to 53 percent in 2005, which suggests that data quality problems are getting worse.

Without a through understanding of data, any extract, transform, and load (ETL) process is doomed to stall in the "code, load, and explode" cycle. The ETL industry only propelled companies into the "code, load, and explode" cycle faster. ETL software helped companies create the extraction and load programs easier, but without a full understanding of the data, bad data was loaded. I have a favorite saying from my data warehouse days: "The good news is we got the data loaded. The bad news is we got the data loaded."

I could go on and on with examples of the costs associated with poor data quality and the reasons why profiling your data is important. Profiling the data before ANY data-related project just makes good business sense. In fact, it makes so much sense that I have had customers "dummy down" their estimated returns on investment (ROI) when analyzing the costs profiling vs. not profiling. Their numbers looked so good that they did not think their management would believe them.

Let's look at some specific examples of data profiling results.

Beage, beige, Bage, Beige, BEIGE

A major auto manufacturer's production records reflected a number of different ways to spell the color "beige." The manufacturer was in the process of moving data into a data warehouse to do decision support. Answers to such critical questions as "How well did beige sell last month?" and "Should we offer a beige car next model year?" depended on how the color "beige" was spelled beige in the query.

Released 11/29/02

When I was associated with a data warehouse vendor, I asked business users what types of questions they wanted to ask of their data. To answer those questions, we looked at the systems that contained the data we thought we'd need to bring into the warehouse. Most of the decisions were made by looking at the documentation and at the system's metadata, or data about the data. We analyzed only a few of the fields – maybe 10 percent – to evaluate the content of the data.

One of the benefits of data profiling is the ability to profile all your data. For example, in a data profiling project for a state department of corrections, almost 90 percent of the comment fields—fields seldom thought of as important—contained a date that an inmate was to be released from prison. Do you think this was important content? The database schema was modified to include this new field.

Shipped vs. Billed

While profiling data, a company looked for relationships between their shipped product data and their billed data. You would expect there would be a 100-percent overlap between the two data sets. What this company found was only a 95-percent overlap. Only 95 percent of the shipped products had been billed. Millions of dollars of shipped product had not billed.

Recently I learned of a company that was paying invoices more than once. When this company realized the duplicates, it found it had paid out millions in overpayments.

There are many other examples of data quality problems, including:

- Products sold but not available in the product catalog
- Commissions paid to an account representative who was no longer an employee
- Debits not equaling credits
- Medicines administered to a patient not admitted to the hospital

You may be reading this and saying to yourself, "These problems cannot happen to my company because we store our data in a relational database management system (RDBMS) that can impose referential integrity." Referential integrity means that, for example, you cannot create a line item for an invoice unless there is an invoice header record. Conversely, if you delete the header record, the database will automatically delete the underlying line items.

The only problem here is that you assume referential integrity was turned on when you initially loaded the database. However, time and time again I see that this assumption is not true. Repeatedly I see that database administrators turn off the referential integrity feature (and other features as well) of the database to get the data loaded. *"The good news is we got the data loaded. The bad news is we got the data loaded."* This is because these database administrators are not charged with looking at the quality of the data before we loading it, and do not have time to do so.

In addition, I find that companies have multiple instances of applications running and cannot reconcile the data between the systems.

While I am sure there are many examples, I know of two specific instances where companies spent millions of dollars developing data warehouses only to have the ultimate users refuse to use the system because the quality of the data was so bad. The system could not answer even the most basic business questions.

What's scarier than spending millions on an unusable data warehouse is the a number of systems out there that are being used on a daily basis and are returning bad information that causes the end user to make questionable business decisions that ultimately cost the business significant revenue.

Feet vs Meters: NASA's Metric Confusion Caused Mars Orbiter Loss

NASA's Climate Orbiter was lost September 23, 1999.

September 30, 1999

(CNN)—NASA lost a $125 million Mars orbiter because one engineering team used metric units while another used English units for a key spacecraft operation, according to a review finding released Thursday.

For that reason, information failed to transfer between the Mars Climate Orbiter spacecraft team at Lockheed Martin in Colorado and the mission navigation team in California. Lockheed Martin built the spacecraft.

"People sometimes make errors," said Edward Weiler, NASA's Associate Administrator for Space Science in a written statement.

"The problem here was not the error, it was the failure of NASA's systems engineering, and the checks and balances in our processes to detect the error. That's why we lost the spacecraft."

The findings of an internal peer review panel at NASA's Jet Propulsion Laboratory showed that the failed information transfer scrambled commands for maneuvering the spacecraft to place it in orbit around Mars. JPL oversaw the Climate Orbiter mission.

"Our inability to recognize and correct this simple error has had major implications," said JPL Director Edward Stone.

The spacecraft completed a nearly 10-month journey to Mars before it was lost on September 23.

The navigation mishap pushed the spacecraft dangerously close to the planet's atmosphere where it presumably burned and broke into pieces, killing the mission on a day when engineers had expected to celebrate the craft's entry into Mars' orbit.

Climate Orbiter was to relay data from an upcoming mission called Mars Polar Lander, set to set down on Mars in December. Now that mission will relay its data via its own radio and another orbiter.

Both Mars Surveyor spacecraft were designed to help scientists understand Mars' water history and the potential for life in the planet's past. There is strong evidence that Mars was once awash with water, but scientists have no clear answers to where the water went and what drove it away.

NASA has convened three panels to look into what led to the loss of the orbiter, including the internal peer review panel that released the Thursday finding.

This story illustrates one of the issues confronting many businesses today: not knowing the differences between data in different systems. If you are a brewery and you ship your recipe from Dublin to St. Louis to be brewed in the United States, is it clear that your recipe is in gallons or liters? If you are a bank, do you handle transactions in U.S. dollars, euros, or British pounds? If you are talking about salary, are you talking about hourly, weekly, monthly, or yearly? If this type of data resides in separate systems, then these discrepancies are not usually a problem. But if you bring this data into a single system, you need to clear up any potential discrepancies—you need to be sure you are comparing apples to apples.

Sharing Partner Data

You want to make your data available to your trading partners. Who is responsible for the bad decisions someone makes because your data is bad? Who is liable if your data becomes available on the Web through a partner? Here are a few tidbits to consider before you share your data.

EPA Order 5360.1 requires environmental data to be of known quality and defensible. How do you know the quality until you have profiled it in some way and certified the quality?

What legal structures will protect individual's privacy and due process rights; define government and business' liability for errors, system misuse, or failure; and protect against unauthorized access or attack?

California Personal Information and Privacy Act requires businesses to notify an individual when their data has been released. However, if you shared it with a partner, and it was compromised at their location or Web site, how would you know?

Thieves stole a laptop computer containing unencrypted personal and confidential data concerning about 382,000 current and former employees of the Boeing Corporation. That disclosure pushed the total number of data breach victims on the Privacy Rights

Clearinghouse Web site to 100,152,801, said Beth Givens, director of the consumer advocacy group.

I highly recommend that you know and can measure the quality of the data to be shared with your trading partners. Before a single byte is shared, I highly recommend that your lawyer and your partner's lawyer agree on what quality is expected and who is liable if it fails to meet those expectations. If you are on the receiving end of data, I recommend that you profile and quantify its quality before you enter it into your systems. I asked a customer if they validated the data they received from a manufacturer. He asked me if he should go out and scratch off the VIN number on the car. I guess he thought the manufacturer did not make mistakes with their data. I did find questionable VIN numbers in his data.

I know of many companies that purchase data for telemarketing campaigns and have been doing so for years. They pay for this data by the number of records. But when they profiled the data they purchased, a significant number of phone numbers were either missing or invalid. They paid for data they could not use.

How much of the data is accurate? Duplicate? At what cost to you?

Protecting Customer Data

Some customer data should never be shown to customers themselves.

In the comment field, I have seen statements like:

- This guy is a real A**hole. He calls me twice a day and just does not get it.
- When you deliver to this house, watch out for the f**king dog.
- This redneck should not be allowed to breed.

- I do not know what she looks like but I can tell you she must be a blond.

Most companies have internal ratings and other measurements about their customers that should never be shared. Until you profile your data, some of this internal information about your customers is not immediately apparent.

Guarding against exposing customer data is not just a good business practice—it's the law. Some state laws dictate that you cannot allow a customer's name and identifier to be released to the public. An identifier can be an account number, Social Security number, passport number, insurance policy number, mother's maiden name, license numbers, permit, etc. There are federal laws such as HIPPA, Sarbanes-Oxley, and the Financial Services Modernization Act that also cover the unauthorized access, use, copy, and distribution of customer data. New legislation to protect customer data is currently working its way through Congress.

I know of a company that was conducting a blanket search of all fields, looking for a pattern that looked like a Social Security number. This company was doing this search because occasionally their telemarketing reps would stick Social Security numbers in fields they should not. Because of security, the reps were not allowed to see Social Security numbers. But they thought they needed the numbers to process a transaction, so they included them in certain database fields.

If you look at only the metadata or old copybooks, you may not know some data has been added if is not in the documentation. How many times have you seen someone store data in ways or places is was not meant to be stored? I know of a company that stopped storing fishing license numbers and started using the fishing license field to store Social Security numbers. Another company stored Internet passwords in a field in the client contact information file. Can you imagine the damage if this information was made available on the Internet?

Here is another example of the risks associated with exposing sensitive data. Let's say I am in a bar and meet a woman. We have a great time, and she gives me her phone number. She has some reasonable expectations that I will not share her number with anyone else. I enter it into my contacts database. As I am trying to reconcile my contacts database with my Outlook database, I run it through a data quality tool to standardize and match duplicates between the two applications. Then, as I'm writing this book on data profiling, let's say I use a screen shot from the data quality tool to illustrate a point. This particular screen shot includes the woman's name and phone number. What are the implications of that innocent revelation?

Companies regularly demonstrate internal systems to non-employees. They are unintentionally exposing customer data to someone that does not need to see it.

If you do not profile your data, you expose yourself to potential risk by just assuming the metadata is correct. Profiling your data significantly reduces your risk in these and other types of situations.

Chapter 2

WHAT IS DATA PROFILING?

DATA profiling is a process whereby one examines the data available in an existing database or flat file and collects statistics and information about that data. These statistics become the real or true metadata. The purpose of these statistics may be to:

- Find out whether existing data can easily be used for other purposes.
- Give metrics on data quality, including whether the data conforms to company standards.
- Assess the risk involved in integrating data for new applications, including the challenges of joins and merges
- Track data quality over time.
- Compile accurate ETL specifications.
- Assess whether metadata accurately describes the actual values in the source database.
- Understand data challenges early in any data-intensive project in order to avoid surprises later. Finding data problems late in a project can incur significant time delays and project cost overruns.
- Document the systems and provide accurate metadata for future projects.
- Find out exactly what data is contained in an old system. I call this process "data archeology."

Some companies also look at data profiling as a way to involve business users in what traditionally has been an IT function.

Business users can often provide context about the data, giving meaning to columns of data that are poorly defined by metadata and documentation.

Typical types of metadata inferred by data profiling software include:

- **Domain values** determine whether the data in the column conforms to the defined values or range of values it is expected to take. For example, ages of children in kindergarten are expected to be between four and six. An age of seven would be considered out of domain for most parts of the country. A code for flammable materials is expected to be A, B, or C. A code of three would be considered out of domain.
- **Data type** identifies character, numeric, date, money, etc.
- **Patterns,** such as a phone number should be (999) 999-9999.
- **Frequency counts;** for example most of our customers should be on the West coast, so the largest number of occurrences of state code should be CA, OR, and WA.
- **Statistics, including:**
  - o Minimum value
  - o Maximum value
  - o Mean value
- **Interdependency, such as:**
  - o Within a table: the account name field is always dependent on the account code field.
  - o Between tables: the sales person number on an order should always appear in the employee table.

Most software vendors divide the data profiling process into three categories: column profiling, dependency profiling, and redundancy profiling. Not all vendors call these categories by these names, but the process occurs in three steps, which can (and, depending on vendor, *must*) be executed in order. Figure 2.1 depicts the process I call the three-dimensional analysis of profiling.

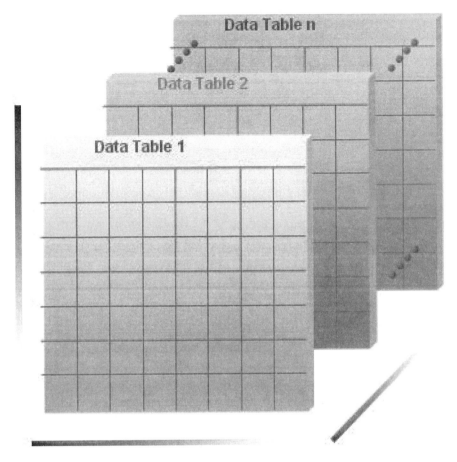

Figure 2.1

Data profiling performs three-dimensional analysis. This involves three main steps:

1. **Column profiling,** including the statistics and domain examples provided above.
2. **Dependency profiling,** which assists in identifying intra-table dependencies. Dependency profiling is related to the normalization of a data source and addresses whether or not there are non-key attributes that determine or are dependent on other non-key attributes. The existence of transitive dependencies here may be evidence of second-normal form.

3. **Redundancy profiling,** which identifies overlapping values between tables. This is typically used to identify candidate foreign keys within tables, to validate attributes that should be foreign keys (but that may not have constraints to enforce integrity), and to identify other areas of data redundancy. For example, redundancy analysis could reveal the fact that the ZIP field in table A contains the same values as the ZIP_code field in table B 80 percent of the time.

Data profiling is the best way to minimize your risk and accelerate your project. Take a look at Figure 2.2. Regarding an upcoming project, you might say to your boss that you can do it better, faster, or cheaper, but pick only two. The idea is if you increase the quality and get the project done faster, it will require more resources, and therefore it will be more expensive. Alternatively, if your boss wants is done cheaper, it may not be as good, or the project will take longer.

Figure 2.2

Well, with an automated data profiling tool, you don't have to pick only two—you get all three. Your project will be better because you will profile all the data, not just a sample (although some vendors will suggest you profile a sample because their software can not handle large volumes of data) or a subset of the fields you need to profile. You can find referential integrity issues before you begin to load the data. You can identify data abnormalities and data type mismatches.

It will be faster because most of the work is done by a computer, not by hand by someone or multiple people writing SAS programs or SQL statements.

Finally, it will be less expensive because you will require fewer resources on the project because you will not find issues months into the project. You will not experience the "code, load, and explode" problem requiring further analysis and rework. Larry English likes to call this "scrape and rework."

Chapter 3

GETTING STARTED

SO how do you start to profile your data? Well, getting started is pretty simple. First, I suggest you purchase a data profiling tool.

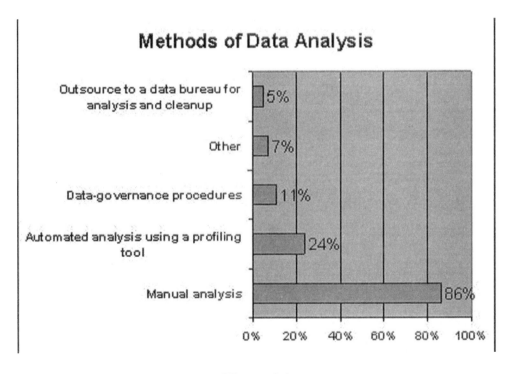

Figure 3.1

As you can see from Figure 3.1, you are not alone if you have not yet purchased a data profiling tool. This chart was published in a TDWI report *"Taking Data Quality to the Enterprise through Data Governance"* in March of 2006 by Philip Russom. As it shows, manual analysis is still the most prevalent method. But this is quickly changing.

It is not the purpose of this book to sell you a profiling tool. I only want to point out that the return on your investment is significant In fact, the ROI on data profiling tools usually looks too good to be true. I recently assisted two companies in defining their ROI on profiling tools. Both companies significantly modified (lowered) their ROI estimates because they did not think their management would believe them.

Once you purchase a data profiling tool, you need to look at the people, processes, and technology required for a profiling project. The people that need to be involved in the project include individuals from both the IT side and the business side. You need to understand the process that will need to be put in place to profile your data. Finally, you need to know how the technology fits into that process.

PEOPLE

The people involved in a data profiling project depend, in part, on the project's type and complexity. For example, a data quality project may not need an ETL developer if the data is never going to leave the existing application. Instead of establishing hard and fast rules about project team members, I will instead identify the different job functions that should be involved and let you decide who you need on your team.

Executive Sponsor

Executive sponsorship is critical to the profiling project's success. The executive sponsor should represent the group that is the ultimate beneficiary of the completed project. If you are doing a Master Data Management (MDM) project with customer data, who is the ultimate beneficiary? Maybe it's the marketing department, which benefits from better direct marketing campaigns? Maybe it's the sales department, which benefits from more accurate customer relationships? Maybe it's the shipping department, which benefits from more accurate delivery information? Maybe it's the accounting department, which benefits from more accurate billing and better collections of accounts receivable? Whichever department is the ultimate beneficiary of the data profiling project's outcome, the highest ranking executive in that organization should be involved in the kick-off and status meetings to make sure the project stays on track. This person is usually easy to find. The money for the project usually comes out of his or her budget. Without an executive sponsor and detailed success criteria linked back to a business imperative, the project is doomed before it even starts.

Business User

The business user or business analyst is the one to make all the ultimate decisions in the project. He or she is the most knowledgeable about the data, its meaning, and how it is used throughout the organization. This person determines what data anomalies are and what to do about them. He or she should know about the different types of customers. What are the ramifications if a customer is not properly categorized? I like to say that the null stops here. When you find a null in the data, this person determines how it should be transformed when you move or cleanse the data.

The business user is usually the person who explains to me the valid exceptions to a business rule. I usually get a rule from the IT department and then find the exceptions in the data. The business user explains to me that, for example, in the year of the flood, people east of the river, older then twenty-one at the time, and planning a career in law enforcement were temporarily exempt if they filed a 21D-CY Revision Three form. I am sure you all have similar exceptions to some of your business rules.

Database Administrator (DBA)

The DBA is a good source of information about the underlying structure of the data. What are the database keys? What are the natural keys? What fields are indexed and why? They can validate a lot of the metadata. Are nulls allowed? Why is the date field a VarChar (13)? The DBA can tell you if referential integrity is turned on. What are some of the rules to maintain the integrity of the data? Are there stored procedures that are triggered upon creating or deleting a record? The DBA is usually the first person I work with because he or she gets me access to the data to profile and helps me validate some of my initial findings.

Extract, Transform, and Load (ETL) Developer

I like to include the ETL developer because he or she can help you make decisions of how to handle validations and transformations. Should we build a reference table or hardcode the validations? Do reference tables already exist from a previous project? What issues might affect the performance of the process? It also gives the ETL developer the opportunity to understand the ramifications of decisions he or she used to make in a vacuum.

While not critical to the project, the ETL developer helps ensure a smoother transition from analysis to movement of the data.

As mentioned earlier, depending on the type of project, an ETL developer may not be needed. If it is a data archeology project, then this person is usually not needed. However, sometimes even in a data archeology project, this person is needed to get the data. Let's say, for example, that I need to access data from the mainframe. The automated profiling tool does not have direct access to the mainframe system. I need the ETL developer to pull the data out of that system and send it to the server so I can profile it as a flat file. I need to make sure that the ETL developer does not do anything during the extraction process that changes the data. I need the ETL developer to expand binary fields and unpack decimal fields, but do not want him or her to change the representation of the data in other ways.

Application Developer

The application developer will also have a wealth of knowledge regarding the underlying data. Are there fields that will default to certain values if not entered by the agent? Are there business rules that are enforced within the application that need to be tested for in data received from outside sources or in the new application or repository? Should these business rules be incorporated into the data quality scorecard to make sure they are not violated once the data leaves the application?

The application developer person is usually the second person I go to with questions about the data. He or she can answer more questions than the DBA unless most of the business rules have been implemented in triggers in the database.

Profiling Facilitator

A facilitator is someone who is skillful in helping a group of people understand their common objectives and plan to achieve them without personally taking any side of the argument. The facilitator will try to assist the group in achieving a consensus on any disagreements that preexist or emerge in the meeting so that it has a strong basis for future action.

This is a person who might be the most "hands on" with the tool. He or she might do the initial profiling, trying to spot the anomalies before anyone else gets involved. He or she might run the discovery sessions, helping to document the issues uncovered, asking questions of all the other team players, soliciting their input, doing typical project management functions, and doing the follow-up to make sure the documented issues are ultimately resolved.

Data Steward

This is a more recent job function, and many companies have not implemented it yet. If this role is new to you, here is one definition:

The data steward is the person responsible for a data standard. A data steward is charged by management to develop and maintain the data standard and to counsel personnel on the proper use of the data. He or she must have a thorough knowledge of the subject matter of the standard, provide accurate and current electronic copies of data relevant to the standard, and weigh the pros and cons of comments received during review of the standard. The data steward is authorized to defend or modify the standard as necessary in order to ensure its proper use.

The data steward should be on the business side of the house but have some typical IT skills like knowledge of SQL and database administration. He or she might even have data modeling skills. The core knowledge is all about the business, the applications, and the underlying data within those applications. Sometimes, this person replaces the business user, as discussed earlier.

Data Stewards

Written by Bill Inmon
Published on February 1, 2007

What is the role of a data steward?

Data stewardship is a position that comes with the maturity of the information resource management environment. When organizations are first designing and building their information management infrastructure, there is nothing for the data stewards to steward. It is kind of like a shepherd without a flock. With no sheep, it is hard for the shepherd to justify his/ her existence.

But as the information infrastructure grows and matures, the little sheep start to pop up, and soon there is a need for data stewards.

So exactly what do data stewards do?

In a word, data stewards tend the data. For the most part, this means that data stewards look after the physical well-being of the data. The data steward is the person you go to when a data set needs to be found. The data steward is the person you go to when the database goes down and it needs to be brought back up. The data steward is the person you go to when a database load program has failed to execute.

In many ways, the job (or at least parts of the job) of the database administrator has morphed into the data steward. There is so much data and so many things happening to the data that we now need data stewards.

So what doesn't the data steward do? The data steward is not responsible for the design of the data or the databases. That job is done long before the data steward comes onto the scene. The data steward does not have the responsibility for the accuracy of the data content. If it is found that in a database, Mr. Jones' first initial is "H," not "A," then it is the responsibility of the applications manager to make that correction. If it is determined that a new column needs to be added to a table, then it is the responsibility of a database administrator to make that change.

The data steward has the job of tending the sheep, not buying them, selling them, or becoming a veterinarian.

One of the big challenges to data stewardship is the sheer volume of data – both the number of bytes and the number of databases that there are to be managed. Once—in the good old days—there were only a few databases and data sets to be managed. In those days, the data steward had the luxury of being able to give individual attention to databases. But today there are so many databases that the data steward has to live in a world of triage. In a world of triage, the data steward must look after data and databases on a basis of monitoring the vital signs of the database. There are standard vital signs—measurements and properties—that are associated with the successful running of a database such as that of running out of capacity, batch loads that fail to execute properly, data exceptions that occur upon access of data inside the database, and so forth.

In a world of thousands of databases—where something can go wrong at any moment—the data steward must monitor the vital signs of each of the databases under his / her care. In many ways, one may be reminded of a control panel such as that found at the helm of the starship Galactica: the control panel shows the vital signs of hundreds and thousands of databases whose vital signs are being monitored.

Another important tool of the data steward is metadata. Metadata allows the data steward to navigate through data efficiently and accurately. Without metadata, the data steward is like Captain Kirk without a compass (or whatever navigation devices one uses in outer space). Metadata simply is an outright necessity for the data steward. It is the shepherd's crook of data stewardship.

As you can see, metadata is critical for the data steward. And true metadata derived from profiling the data is the only way to go.

Data Modeler

The data modeler's job is defined as:

The analysis of data objects and their relationships to other data objects. Data modeling is often the first step in database design and object-oriented programming as the designers first create a conceptual model of how data items relate to each other. Data modeling involves a progression from conceptual model to logical model to physical schema.

The data modeler should know the structure of the source systems and help validate the structure that the profiling discovers. The data modeler should also help make decisions to affect the structure of the output of the modeling or mappings to the ultimate target system. For example, the profiling might determine that there are two potential keys to a table. The modeler might help decide which one should be the primary key. In addition, if hidden tables are identified, he or she might help decide if this hidden table should be normalized or leave it denormalized.

This should give you a good idea of who should be invited to the party. Not every project will require all of these functions, but at least you now know who might be required on your project team. One thing to keep in mind is that each of these roles can be combined. For example, the business user or the data Steward might also be the facilitator. In addition, depending on the size of the project, you may need multiple members from each of the functional areas involved. Another possibility is that one person may represent one or more of the roles described above.

In some cases, I have found that a more traditional project manager is also involved. However, the project manager is usually part of a greater business initiative of which data profiling plays an important part. In this case, the facilitator usually reports the status of the data profiling portion of the project and other required information back to the project manager.

PROCESS

Let us take a quick look at the process of data profiling.

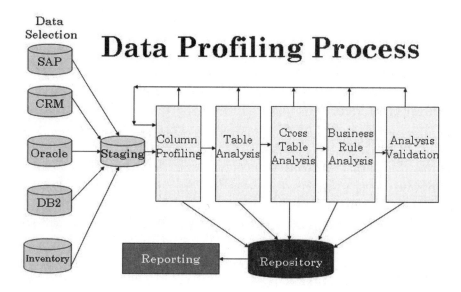

Figure 3.2

As Figure 3.2 depicts, there are eight main steps involved in data profiling. Although not all eight are always required, the steps are:

1. Data selection
2. Staging or direct access
3. Column profiling
4. Table analysis
5. Cross table analysis
6. Business rules
7. Analysis validation
8. Reporting

Data Selection

Once you identify your project team members, the first step is to identify the data you need to profile.

In identifying the data you will be profiling, your first consideration is the end result of your project. If you are doing a Master Data Management (MDM) project involving customer data, then you start with customer data. If you are planning to bring multiple customer systems together, you should start with a single system. Profile that system and make sure you can normalize it before you add another system.

If you need help in deciding which system to start with, I suggest you pick the one you think will be the easiest or the one to which you can get quick access to the data. I have seen projects delayed because getting the data becomes the bottleneck. Either the application owner is difficult to deal with, or the data extraction is complex and requires specialized skills to get it. If access is not an issue, then pick the system that you think will be easiest because the application knowledge is readily available or the data is perceived to be cleanest. It is always good to get some early success and show progress in the project. And most projects have a learning curve, so it is better to start with the most readily accessible, cleanest, least problematic data to demonstrate momentum quickly.

Once you identify the data you want to profile, you then need to know how you will group your data together. Common grouping methods are by subject or source system. If you are trying only to understand a source system, then a source system method makes the most sense. If you are trying a MDM project for customer, then you will need to bring all the different sources of customer data together in one project. If this is a Product Information Management (PIM) project, then you need to find all the product records and bring them into the project.

Here are a few words of caution. You should work on one source at a time to understand what you are looking at. You should also be aware that some profiling tools do not allow you to add sources

45

once you select your data. Once you select the tables to profile, you cannot go back and add additional tables.

If you are starting a data quality initiative, you can do group your data either by subject or source. The reason I say you can do it by subject is that you will start developing subject matter expertise on a particular subject and can immediately apply it to additional systems as you bring in the data. In addition, you may want to go back and do further analysis on sources you already profiled because you learned something new with the addition of the next system.

As you profile more systems, you learn more. You add to the valid value set. Let's look at an example. Let's say you are an insurance company and are trying to bring together customer data for an MDM project. One line of your business operates mainly in the northeast, and another line operates business predominately in the south. Adding to the valid states in which you do business changes from line of business to line of business, but you want to develop one set of valid values for all your lines of business.

If you group your data by source system, you have the benefit of having the application expert or subject matter expert in the room who can answer all your questions at one time regarding all the tables. If you group it by subject, you have to keep bring in different application experts or subject matter experts for each system. In addition, you'd need to call the same subject matter expert multiple times as you move from subject to subject.

If you were working on a data warehouse project, you would probably group your data subject by subject as you build out the warehouse.

Staging or Direct Access

Once you select the data you intend to profile, you need to decide if you are going to stage the data in a separate database, profile it in its existing location, or profile it as flat files on the profiling server. Each option has its pros and cons.

Profiling is a very resource-intensive process. You may not want to profile the data in an existing transaction processing system during prime time. But thanks to the Internet and globalization, most transaction processing systems operate 24/7. As a result, you may have to extract data into a staging area to do the profiling. If you are going to do this, I recommend that you use your backup, which allows you to profile your data while testing your backup and recovery procedures at the same time.

If there is downtime on the transaction processing system, you could schedule the data profiling then. Some profiling tools have a batch capability, which can be scheduled with an ETL or workflow tool. If the system is not a transaction processing system – like a data warehouse, for example – then you could profile it right where it is. If the data resides on a mainframe, it is usually extracted to either flat files or a staging system and imported into a relational database.

Depending on the profiling tool you select, you may have only one option. For example, some tools profile only the data on their profiling server. You must move the data to their server and profile it there. Even if it is in a relational database, the software does a full table scan and moves it across the network and profiles it on the server. Another vendor's software requires it to be moved to their priority database for analysis. Still other data profiling tools make use of the underlying database, using the power of the database server to help in the profiling process.

The latter is my favorite because you get the best of both worlds, and you are not required to do one or the other. You can profile the analytical system without moving it and stage the transaction processing system. Because this method uses the database as well as the profiling server, you get to spread the processing around and get the job done much faster without having to replicate the data across the network.

Column Analysis

The next step in the data profiling process is column analysis. This process involves extracting details about each column in a table. It returns true metadata because it is based on the data itself. You get information like:

- Distinct values and frequency distribution of values
- Data type
- Nulls rule, percentage of nulls, the number of nulls
- Inferred data type
- Frequency distribution of patterns
- Minimum, mean, and maximum values

In Figure 3.3, you can see an example of the results of column analysis.

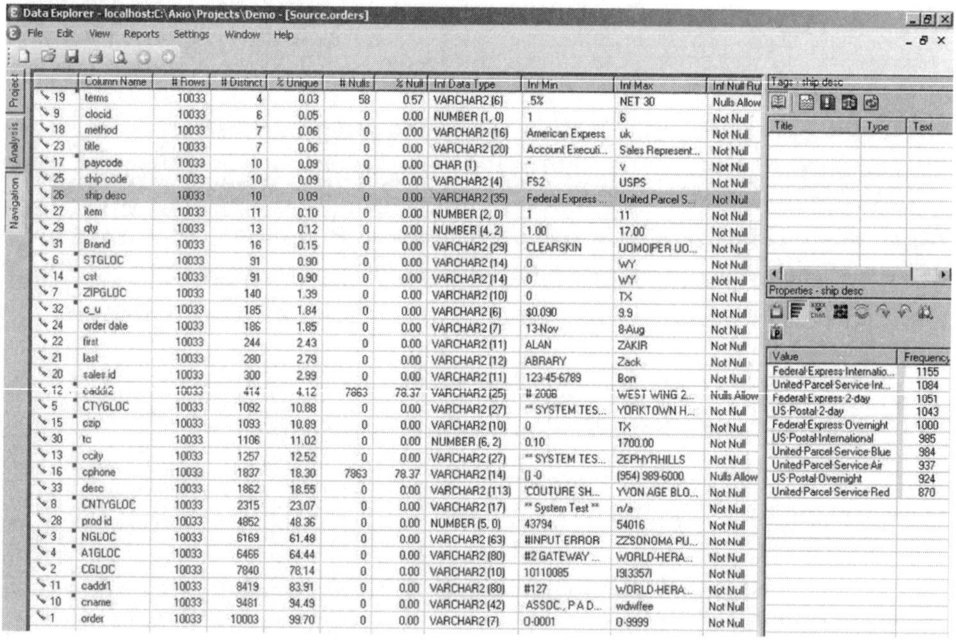

	Column Name	# Rows	# Distinct	% Unique	# Nulls	% Null	Inf Data Type	Inf Min	Inf Max	Inf Null Rul
19	terms	10033	4	0.03	58	0.57	VARCHAR2 (6)	.5%	NET 30	Nulls Allow
9	clocid	10033	6	0.05	0	0.00	NUMBER (1, 0)	1	6	Not Null
18	method	10033	7	0.06	0	0.00	VARCHAR2 (16)	American Express	uk	Not Null
23	title	10033	7	0.06	0	0.00	VARCHAR2 (20)	Account Executi...	Sales Represent...	Not Null
17	paycode	10033	10	0.09	0	0.00	CHAR (1)	*	v	Not Null
25	ship code	10033	10	0.09	0	0.00	VARCHAR2 (4)	FS2	USPS	Not Null
26	ship desc	10033	10	0.09	0	0.00	VARCHAR2 (35)	Federal Express ...	United Parcel S...	Not Null
27	item	10033	11	0.10	0	0.00	NUMBER (2, 0)	1	11	Not Null
29	qty	10033	13	0.12	0	0.00	NUMBER (4, 2)	1.00	17.00	Not Null
31	Brand	10033	16	0.15	0	0.00	VARCHAR2 (29)	CLEARSKIN	UOMOIPER UO...	Not Null
6	STGLOC	10033	91	0.90	0	0.00	VARCHAR2 (14)	0	WY	Not Null
14	cst	10033	91	0.90	0	0.00	VARCHAR2 (14)	0	WY	Not Null
7	ZIPGLOC	10033	140	1.39	0	0.00	VARCHAR2 (10)	0	TX	Not Null
32	c_u	10033	185	1.84	0	0.00	VARCHAR2 (6)	$0.090	9.9	Not Null
24	order date	10033	186	1.85	0	0.00	VARCHAR2 (7)	13-Nov	8-Aug	Not Null
22	first	10033	244	2.43	0	0.00	VARCHAR2 (11)	ALAN	ZAKIR	Not Null
21	last	10033	280	2.79	0	0.00	VARCHAR2 (12)	ABRARY	Zack	Not Null
20	sales id	10033	300	2.99	0	0.00	VARCHAR2 (11)	123-45-6789	Bon	Not Null
12	caddr2	10033	414	4.12	7863	78.37	VARCHAR2 (25)	# 2008	WEST WING 2...	Nulls Allow
5	CTYGLOC	10033	1092	10.88	0	0.00	VARCHAR2 (27)	** SYSTEM TES...	YORKTOWN H...	Not Null
15	czip	10033	1093	10.89	0	0.00	VARCHAR2 (10)	0	TX	Not Null
30	tc	10033	1106	11.02	0	0.00	NUMBER (6, 2)	0.10	1700.00	Not Null
13	ccity	10033	1257	12.52	0	0.00	VARCHAR2 (27)	** SYSTEM TES...	ZEPHYRHILLS	Not Null
16	cphone	10033	1837	18.30	7863	78.37	VARCHAR2 (14)	() -0	(954) 989-6000	Nulls Allow
33	desc	10033	1862	18.55	0	0.00	VARCHAR2 (113)	'COUTURE SH...	YVON AGE BLO...	Not Null
8	CNTYGLOC	10033	2315	23.07	0	0.00	VARCHAR2 (17)	** System Test **	n/a	Not Null
28	prod id	10033	4852	48.36	0	0.00	NUMBER (5, 0)	43794	54016	Not Null
3	NGLOC	10033	6169	61.48	0	0.00	VARCHAR2 (63)	#INPUT ERROR	ZZSONOMA PU...	Not Null
4	A1GLOC	10033	6466	64.44	0	0.00	VARCHAR2 (80)	#2 GATEWAY ...	WORLD-HERA...	Not Null
2	CGLOC	10033	7840	78.14	0	0.00	VARCHAR2 (10)	10110085	I913357I	Not Null
11	caddr1	10033	8419	83.91	0	0.00	VARCHAR2 (80)	#127	WORLD-HERA...	Not Null
10	cname	10033	9481	94.49	0	0.00	VARCHAR2 (42)	ASSOC., P A D...	wdwffee	Not Null
1	order	10033	10003	99.70	0	0.00	VARCHAR2 (7)	0-0001	0-9999	Not Null

Value	Frequency
Federal Express Internatio...	1155
United Parcel Service Int...	1084
Federal Express 2-day	1051
US Postal 2-day	1043
Federal Express Overnight	1000
US Postal International	985
United Parcel Service Blue	984
United Parcel Service Air	937
US Postal Overnight	924
United Parcel Service Red	870

Figure 3.3

Some systems will compare the documented metadata, such as data type, null rule, and minimum and maximum values if available, to the inferred values and highlight the differences. This comparison helps you identify potential problems with your metadata. If you built your target based upon your source metadata, you can run into problems trying to load the data. A simple example is the null rule. Your target is based upon your documentation that says nulls are not allowed, but you have 4.41 percent nulls in your data. What if your data is a Char 10 data type, but the data was inferred as a date? While this discrepancy doesn't prevent you from loading your data, you might want to consider storing the data as a date field.

Table Analysis

The next step in the process is table analysis. This is where you look at the structure of the table, one table at a time. In a perfect world, there is a single determinant, and all the other fields are dependent on that column. In a database world, you are looking for the primary key.

A determinant means that for any one value in the determinant field, there will be one and only one value in the dependent field. Let us look at an example in Table 3.1.

Customer_ID	Name	Phone
12345	Ed	555.831.1234
34678	Tim	555.448.1234
24804	Lynn	555.567.1234
14268	Deana	555.226.1234
29966	Tim	555.678.1234
28736	Dave	555.334.1234
12345	Ed	555.831.4321

Table 3.1

In this example, Customer_ID is the determinant for name. You see two Customer_IDs 12345 that both point to Ed. You may see that Customer_ID 34567 and 29966 both point to Tim. However, when you look at the phone numbers, you see they are different. Customer_ID is not the determinant for phone. You observe that Customer_ID 12345 points to two different phone numbers. You notice that the phone number is a determinant for both Customer_ID and Name because the phone number is unique in this small sample of data. In a situation like this you need a subject matter expert to help you ascertain what is a business fact and what is a coincidence in the data.

Depending on what you are trying to achieve, you may or may not perform table analysis. This step verifies your keys and looks for subtables and assists in the normalization process. Many databases are denormalized for a number of good reasons, such as performance, ease of reporting, etc. However, many older databases were never normalized in the first place.

Table analysis helps you to normalize these tables. There was a time when the main output in the data profiling process was to generate a third normal form of the data to help build the target schema. Now, most data migration projects involve moving data to an enterprise application like Seibel, PeopleSoft, Oracle, or SAP. This step is still used, but now I see companies trying to normalize an older system into a staging area before moving the data into the new application. Before you move the data from an old mainframe system to a new application, you need to understand the structure of the data.

Figure 3.4 shows an example of dependencies that exist within the table. Many of the results are a function of the sample size and coincidences in the data. For example, paycode is a determinant for cphone, method, and terms.

	Determinants	Dependent	Validation	In Model
17	order	first	True	
18	order	title	True	
19	order	order date	True	
20	order	ship code	True	
21	order	ship desc	True	
22	order	Brand	True	
23	A1GLOC	cphone	True	
24	CTYGLOC	cphone	True	
25	STGLOC	cphone	True	
26	ZIPGLOC	cphone	Gray	
27	CNTYGLOC	cphone	True	
28	cname	clocid	True	
29	cname	cphone	True	
30	cname	paycode	Gray	
31	cname	method	Gray	
32	cname	terms	Gray	
33	cname	Brand	True	
34	caddr1	A1GLOC	True	
35	caddr1	clocid	True	
36	caddr1	cphone	True	
37	ccity	CTYGLOC	Gray	
38	ccity	clocid	Gray	
39	ccity	cphone	True	
40	czip	ZIPGLOC	True	
41	czip	cphone	True	
42	paycode	cphone	True	
43	paycode	method	True	
44	paycode	terms	True	
45	method	cphone	True	
46	method	terms	True	
47	terms	cphone	Gray	
48	sales id	cphone	True	
49	sales id	last	True	
50	sales id	first	True	
51	sales id	title	True	

Figure 3.4

Cross-Table Analysis

The next step in the process is cross-table analysis. Cross-table analysis looks for relationships that exist between tables. This is done by comparing the distinct values in each column with the distinct values of every other column of every table you load into a project. You can also selectively pick the columns you wish to compare.

This step is sometimes called redundancy analysis because of the percentage of overlap (or redundancy) of the values between column pairs. Normally, you look for primary key–foreign key relationships. If you are working on a MDM or PIM project, you also look for duplicate data. If you are trying to bring three instances of vehicle data, you also find columns in the different tables with the same business facts like color, model, engine size, number of doors, mileage, etc.

51

It's important to consider not only what profiling tools show you about relationships, but also what they do not show you. Let me give you an example. I worked with a large financial services company, which gave me its customer tables from different business units (different systems). I ran cross-table analysis and showed the company the results. The software did not find any significant overlap between the state columns in their three tables. The company complained about the software's performance. But when I showed them the actual values contained in the three columns, they were stunned. One table had county codes, one had two character state codes, and the last one had the full state name. Their intent was to move the data into a new warehouse "as is." Another company would have fallen victim to the dreaded "code, load, and explode" phenomenon.

Business Rules

Once you have done your initial profiling, you may want to build business rules to further test your assumptions about the data or explore more detailed data quality issues. Here is a more detailed business rule to test the quality of the data in a loan application:

```
(UPPER (LOAN_TYPE) = 'AUTO' and
(LOAN_AMT not between 3000 and 50000 or
LOAN_TERM not between 12 and 60))
Or
(UPPER (LOAN_TYPE) = 'REAL' and
(LOAN_AMT not between 10000 and 500000 or
LOAN_TERM not between 36 and 360))
Or
LOAN_TYPE is null or LOAN_AMT is null or
LOAN_TERM is null
```

In this example, we may also be looking at what appear to be anomalies, drilling further into the records to determine if they are anomalies, and trying to figure out the cause of the anomalies. If I find negative numbers in a column, what is the reason? Building a business rule might simply result in showing me all the negative numbers that do not have a reason code of RTN. Alternatively, I may want to test my assumptions that I know are true. Show me all the vehicle identification numbers that have a U, Z, or O in model year since these would be invalid.

Let's consider an example of business rules in action. I have been working with a large retail pharmacy chain. This chain has over six thousand stores with individual systems in each store. They are moving to a centralized system. They want to profile the data from all the stores except they do not want to bring it in at one time. They plan to profile the data from a hundred or two hundred stores at a time.

I showed them how to profile the first set of stores and build a valid set of domain values for most of the fields. Then I built a set of business rules to validate against the data from those stores and set it up to run against the next set of stores. The results kicked out any records that were not contained in the value set. The analyst then worked with the business or application subject matter expert to validate the exceptions. If the exceptions were correct, they were added to the business rule so that the next set of stores benefited from the enhanced business knowledge.

An example might be the one mentioned earlier – the large retail pharmacy chain. Valid state codes from the first set of files generate a valid set of values. Since each of the stores does business in only a limited number of states, the initial set of values is small. As they move from region to region, they add additional states as they encounter them.

I know, in real life this may be a bad example because I could just add the USPS table of valid state codes. I use it only to show how the process might work. A real example would be competitor codes. Each store would have a limited set of competitors. As you move from store to store, you have different competitors.

Analysis Validation

Analysis validation is the next step in the process. As you go through the steps of profiling your data, you make many decisions regarding the content, structure, and quality of your data. Most of these decisions are built on sample data and domain values.

You need to be aware of some issues associated with the automated analysis. When deciding on a key for a table, the software bases its analysis on sample data. If the relationship does not exist in the sample, it will never exist in the full population of the data. However, just because it exits in the sample, it may not exist in the full population of the data.

The same is true of cross-table analysis. It is based on the 16,000 most frequent values. If you have a table of a million rows or more and the column is unique, you are missing many values. This is where analysis validation comes in. Data profiling software helps you quickly validate your analysis. Some validation steps include:

- Key analysis
- Join analysis
- Vertical merge analysis
- Primary key—foreign key analysis
- Duplicate record analysis

We will explore these validation steps in much greater detail in a later chapter.

Reporting

Once you do all your profiling and build all your business rules, you can run these rules repeatedly against your data. You need a reporting mechanism for your results. Most results are stored in a relational database. Most vendors supply reports to run against this repository, but I am seeing more and more companies generate custom reports with business intelligence (BI) tools run against the repository. In the example of the retail pharmacy, the chain wanted one report to show the consolidated values for each field across all of their analysis. This required a customized report to consolidate all the profiling results from the different set of stores.

It is also becoming commonplace to convert the results of the business rules into scorecards. Building scorecards is really a method of measuring the quality of the data. Each business rule generates a result. You can aggregate your results and add a weighting factor for rules or fields that are more important than others. By keeping results run over time, you can see how you data quality either improves or deteriorates over time.

Reporting is not really part of data profiling. I only mention it because once you finish profiling and testing your business rules, you many want to have a mechanism to provide feedback to those who supplied the data in the first place to monitor your data quality results. This is especially important if you plan to run the rules on a regular basis.

Some data profiling tools include a mapping capability. After you profile your sources, you can import the target schema. Using a drag-and-drop capability, you map the source fields to the target. In the process, the software compares the metadata and highlights any potential mismatches in the metadata. In addition, it creates source-to-target or target-to-source maps. The good thing about these maps is that all of the tags are included in the maps. Tags will be discussed in great length later in this book.

These maps are great for giving the ETL developer near-perfect specifications for doing their job, rather then relying on the metadata and documentation to generate the ETL rules. Remember the example of the financial services company that had three different ways of storing the state? This company hired a consulting firm to put together their project plan for moving the data from the three applications into one centralize system. The consultants were working independently from the rest of the team and were basing all of their decisions on documentation and COBOL copybooks.

The mapping reports are also great for compliance requirements. They document what should have happened and what the process and rules were at the time.

TECHNOLOGY

When you decide to profile your data, you also have to make some decisions about technology. For example, which operating system do you plan to use? What kind of naming conventions will you use? What type of security requirements do you have? I will walk you through the different choices and issues associated with each of them to help you make your decisions.

Operating System (OS)

There are a couple of things to consider before you decide which OS to use. First, does your profiling tool run on your preferred OS? I know it sounds silly, but I have seen companies moving along with a project, assuming they can run the software on their favorite OS, only to come to a screeching halt when it does not. While most tools run on the major OSs, such as Windows, AIX, Solaris, and HP-UX, you still need to check. For example, do you require Linux?

Another consideration, of course, is what is your company's standard? Can you only run on the corporate standard of AIX? Is Windows an issue for you? Do you require 64 bit architecture?

Once these OS considerations are taken into account, then you want to look at performance. If you plan to profile a large amount of data over an extended period of time (years instead of months), you need to consider performance. If you are planning a system greater than four processors, I recommend considering UNIX or Linux. In addition, you might look at Blades or grid technology. These options will also affect your OS decision.

My first choice is always UNIX. It is rock solid, and it gives you the best performance. It also has very good security, which will be discussed later in this chapter.

Naming Conventions

Naming conventions are usually the last thing the project team thinks about. Usually a month after the project is started and things are getting out of hand is when naming conventions are discussed. Consider setting up standard naming conventions for things like project names, tags, and validations.

Project Names

> You need to consider what to name a project. Do you name it after the source(s), target(s), overall project name, data subject name?
>
> When you begin your project, do you keep all the projects in one directory, or does each user keep their projects in their own directory? All projects in one directory make sharing among the team members easier and aids in backing up the results. If the projects are spread out over multiple directories, it becomes harder to find the analysis you are looking for.
>
> Security is part of the decision. For example, do you need to lock down a particular subject, like personnel records, so only one or two people are able to see it? If you plan to keep all the projects in one area, then you need to have a standardized method of naming the projects so you know what is contained in the project and you do not have contention with project names.
>
> If you have multiple projects going on simultaneously, you might want to start with an abbreviation of the project name, followed by either the source system name or subject area name. You can also date the project in case you plan to profile the same data over multiple time periods. Adding a date also lets you know how fresh the analysis is just by looking at the project name. Here is one example.

DW-CUST-1207

If multiple project team members need to view the results of each system, you may choose to name the projects simply by source system. In so doing, you allow other people in your organization who are working on other data-related projects to view the results of an analysis by simply opening the project and viewing the analysis results.

If you name your projects by the target, it may be more difficult for other people in your organization who are working on other data-related projects to know the sources you profiled. However, if the target eventually becomes a source for other projects, this will assist those people in understanding how the data in the system was initially built. You may still need to reprofile the data to see if any new data problems have crept into the system, but at least you have a baseline to compare your results to the original profiling.

My favorite naming convention method is to name the project after the source system, if possible.

Tags

Naming conventions need to be addressed for standardizing tags. As you will learn, tags are those notes, action items, business rules, and transformations that are attached to a particular column or table. My personal favorite is to give the tag a name that describes the potential issue that you are investigating. I use questions or statements. "Is this pattern valid?" or "Definitions needed." Alternatively, "Do these values look right to you?"

I have seen others try a naming convention that incorporates several pieces of information into the name: source, column name, date, etc. In most software packages, there are other tag fields where most of the information is provided. I like to have a general idea about what I am looking at before I open the tag. It speeds up the analysis process and helps me find the more critical problems easier.

Validations

In data profiling software, validations are to test certain preconceived or learned facts about the data, such as primary key–foreign key relations and joins.

Joins drive me nuts. The results of a join are the number of records that do not participate in the join. In the case of a vertical merge, the results of a join are the records that do participate in the join. The results are returned in the "parent and child" form. I always forget which table I picked to be the parent and which I picked to be the child. Therefore, the method I use to name all my validations is as follows:

- Key validation—table name.column name, (column name) example: orders.orderid,itemnum
- Primary key–Foreign Key Validation—Primary Key table name.column name,column name- Foreign Key table name.column name, column name Example: Product. productnum-Orders.itemnum
- Join—Parent table name.column name,column name- Child table name.column name,column name Example: Customer.custnum-Orders.custnum
- Vertical Merge—Parent table name.column name, column name- Child table name.column name, column name Example: Employee.empid-NewCo.empnum

This way, when I look at the name, I immediately know who the parent is, who the child is, and what columns participate in the validation.

Security

Security is a big issue for most companies. Some companies will not let their own employees see uncensored data. Two companies I have worked with run Social Security numbers through a filter to transform the number but still create unique values. Another company jumbles the names so you are never looking at an actual customer name. Other companies only let you see the data through views that hide certain columns. Then there is the government. Security is always a big issue with the government.

Let's look at some ways to lock down the profiling environment. However, before we look at ways to enhance security, I want to caution you that every security measure you put in place will further limit the flexibility of your software and your team members.

Some software packages store results in the server file system, while others store data in a RDBMS. If your software stores the results in the file system, you can use the operating system to secure the data. In UNIX, you know you can set read and write permissions for an individual login, group of logins, or anybody that has a login on the system. Therefore, using the operating system, you can lock each project down to the individual or group.

Here is where you limit flexibility. If you lock each project down to an individual, only one person can view the results of the profiling unless the team members share the same login. This violates the concept of setting up security for one user at a time. If you want to lock the profiling down to just the team members, you can allow read–write access to the group instead of the individual. You can also have multiple groups so different users may be able to view some types of data but not others. If the software uses an RDBMS, you can use the RDBMS to provide security, only allowing read–write access to certain individuals or groups.

You also have the ability to limit access to data to be profiled by using either the operating system or the RDBMS. Using the same techniques, you can limit access in the operating system by limiting access to the flat files in the system to individuals, groups, or to the entire team. The same is true of the RDBMS. You can limit access to the individual tables to only certain members of the group or the whole group. You can also create views, hiding certain columns from the profiling exercise.

Some software packages provide for encryption of passwords and traffic between the client and server, which allows for secure transmission of data from different locations to the profile server. All server traffic can be inside the firewall so that the traffic from the profiling server to the data location can be made very secure.

I am sure there are other security concerns, and your environment has its own security issues to deal with. The good thing is most data profiling software can adapt to your security requirements.

Performance Issues

One issue that comes up all the time is performance. How fast can you profile a table? The following equation identifies most of the factors that affect the performance of profiling software.

Profiling Performance = server (speed of processor * number of processors) + amount of available memory + operating system - number of active users of the system – number of active applications + software
release levels
plus
Location of the data (SANS (plus speed of SANS), Or NAS (plus speed of network), Or RAID, Or DAS)* number of controllers)
plus
RDBMS + database server (speed of processor * number of processors) + amount of available memory - number of active users of the system – number of active applications + software
release levels
plus
speed of LAN / WAN + level of encryption
plus
number of records * (number of columns + cardinality of data)
plus
current phase of the moon and if the government is secretly monitoring your systems and network

Performance Test

I did a quick set of tests to examine some of the factors affecting performance of profiling software. This is by no means an exhaustive study, rather a quick glimpse of a couple of simple tests. Figure 3.5 shows a diagram of the performance test environment.

Performance Test Environment

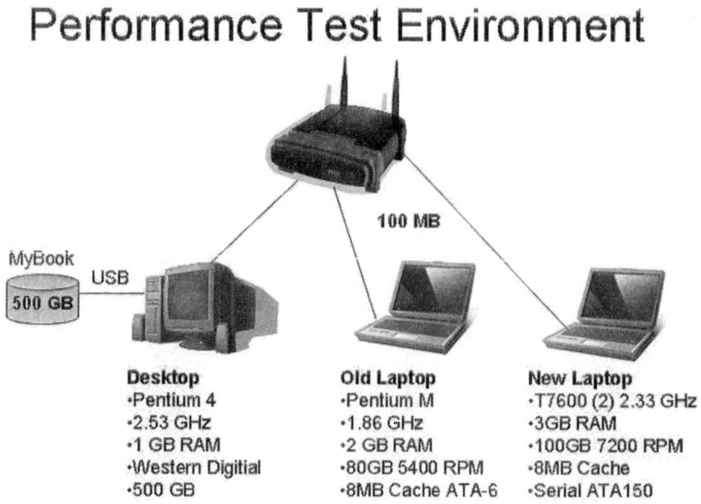

Figure 3.5

Based upon the configuration in Figure 3.5, I set out to test a number of factors:

- CPU speed
- Available RAM
- Location of data
- Client–server ramifications
- Effects of profiling a flat file versus a relational database

The raw results were:

Client	Server	Data Source	Columns	Total Time	Avg. Minutes per Column
Old laptop	Old laptop	Remote Flat File	152 of 413	21 hours	8.29
New Laptop	New Laptop	Remote Flat File	152 of 413	21 hours	8.29
Desktop	Desktop	Local Flat File	152 of 413		3.92
New Laptop	New Laptop	Local Flat File	152 of 413	3 hours 27minutes	1.36
Old laptop	Old laptop	Local Flat File	152 of 413	8 hours 12minutes	3.24
Desktop	New Laptop	Local Flat File	152 of 413	3 hours 42minutes	1.46
New Laptop	New Laptop	SQL Sever	152 of 413	10 hours 58minutes	4.33

Based upon these results we can draw the following conclusions:

1. Location of the data is critical. This is evidenced by the fact that the performance numbers for the old and new laptop were identical even though the new laptop was faster and had a dual-core CPU. If you are profiling flat files, you should load the data on the same system as the profile server. While not shown here, I watched the network traffic, which was at the theoretical maximum during the tests.
2. As evidenced by the desktop performance discrepancies, memory or disk speed was a minor factor in column analysis, while the faster CPU performed slightly than

the old laptop. However, it is also possible there are slight differences in the architecture, local cache, system bus, etc. which can also explain the minor differences. In both cases, the memory required was less than what was available. I suspect the difference in using the local disk on the laptop vs. the USB drive on the desktop was the deciding factor.

3. CPU speed is king. This is evidenced by the speed of the old laptop vs. the new laptop. The new laptop performed more than twice as fast as the old laptop. Although the new laptop is a dual-core machine remember that most profiling software will not use more than one CPU at a time. However, when leaving the additional processor to run the other server processes, offloading the profiling software processor does help.

4. Running in client server mode is better when the server is a faster processor than the client.

5. I am concerned that SQL server as a source ran significantly slower then a flat file. I have run other tests with other databases in the past, and they significantly outperformed the flat file performance. I have profiled billion row tables, but I was using the Teradata system to do a lot of the work.

Chapter 4

SPECIFIC PROFILING TECHNIQUES

WE now turn our attention to techniques to analyze data. In this chapter, we walk through these techniques one at a time. Later we combine them to look at specific types of data, like money fields. After that, we combine them to look at specific business facts like vehicle identification numbers (VIN) and Social Security numbers.

Number of Distinct Values

One of the first things I do when I am profiling data is to sort the results of column profiling by the number of distinct values. I do this for two reasons. The first is to show me all of the fields that are either 100-percent null or are a constant field. A constant field is a column that has one distinct value or one distinct value and nulls.

Recently I was profiling some data from an SAP application. The table had 132 columns. When I sorted by the number of distinct values, 102 columns were either 100-percent null or were a constant field. This helped me quickly identify fields that needed no further work on my part because they were not being used by my customer.

This experience of profiling data from an SAP application is actually quite typical of enterprise application software. It used to be that companies bought these applications and modified them to fit their business requirements. This customization was very expensive. It became even more expensive when the software vendor released a new version or additional modules, and the customization had to be done all over again. Nowadays, most companies forgo the expensive customization and simply populate the schema fields for which they have data and use on a regular basis.

I also like to group the columns by distinct values because it tends to group like values together. For example, if I have a shipping and billing address in the same record, it groups the state columns close together.

Sorting the columns is a quick way to see the quality of your data just by looking at the number of distinct values in a particular column. At the top of the list are all your indicator fields. Let me give you an example of how this is useful. I remember profiling a relatively new application for an insurance company. Sitting next to me, the business analyst was looking down at her documentation and saw the field was a "yes or no" field. The documentation said that it contained a Y or an N. She said we could skip this field. I replied that was okay with me, but I asked her what she wanted to do with the other three values that were in the field. She nearly fell out of her chair.

	Column Name	# Rows	# Distinct	% Unique	# Nulls	% Null	Inf Data Type	Inf Min	Inf Max	Inf Null Rul
1	cust_number	10081	10055	99.74	0	0.00	VARCHAR2 (10)	10,112,285	19133571	Not Null
2	Salutation	10081	0	0.00	10081	100.00				Nulls Allow
3	contact_name	10081	9348	92.72	5	0.04	VARCHAR2 (42)	****DO NOT US...	wdwlfee	Nulls Allow
4	company_n...	10081	7441	73.81	1	0.01	VARCHAR2 (63)	#INPUT ERROR	ZZSONOMA PU...	Nulls Allow
5	address1	10081	8161	80.95	1	0.01	VARCHAR2 (80)	#1 TOMS POIN...	WORLD-HERA...	Nulls Allow
6	address2	10081	1246	12.35	29	0.28	VARCHAR2 (27)	** SYSTEM TES...	ZANESVILLE	Nulls Allow
7	address3	10081	94	0.93	529	5.24	VARCHAR2 (14)	AK	WY	Nulls Allow
8	address4	10081	444	4.40	9407	93.31	VARCHAR2 (10)	10001	TX	Nulls Allow
9	zip_or_post...	10081	2637	26.15	701	6.95	VARCHAR2 (17)	** System Test **	n/a	Nulls Allow
10	iso_ctry_code	10081	9	0.08	228	2.26	VARCHAR2 (13)	(US)	United States	Nulls Allow
11	cust_start_d...	10081	2604	25.83	13	0.12	DATE [dd/mm/y...	1/1/1900	14/12/1994	Nulls Allow
12	currency	10081	13	0.12	324	3.21	VARCHAR2 (21)	#input error	unknown	Nulls Allow
13	cust_turnover	10081	8485	84.16	3	0.02	VARCHAR2 (16)	#input error	unknown	Nulls Allow
14	cust_end_d...	10081	56	0.55	9774	96.95	DATE [dd/mm/y...	25/01/1980	2/6/2003	Nulls Allow
15	cust_status	10081	8	0.07	0	0.00	VARCHAR2 (10)	A	pending	Not Null
16	Last_Order_...	10081	1	0.01	0	0.00	DATE [dd/mm/y...	31/12/99	31/12/99	Not Null

Figure 4.1

Let's look at another example: the address3 field in Figure 4.1 This is the state field, and it has 94 values. There are only 62 valid state codes as defined by the United States Postal Service. By looking at this, you immediately know you have anomalies in the data and would require further investigation.

What about country codes? The United Nations has 191 members but the United States recognizes 192 countries. The International Organization for Standardization (ISO) includes 244 countries in its country table (see list in Appendix).

These values are quantifiable. In which other columns can you use ditinct values to do a quick validation of the data?

- Number of customers–customer ID
- Number of employees–employee ID
- Number of products –product ID
- Books in a library–ISBN
- Number of students–student ID
- Doctors in a hospital–DEA Numbers
- Patients in a hospital–patient ID
- Marines deployed in a country–dog tag number
- Number of cars for a rental car company–VIN number

The numbers do not have to be exact but if the numbers do not look logical or reasonable then you need to do further investigation.

Valid Values

So now, your data looks reasonable but are the values valid? You have 60 state codes, but are the values UK and XX valid? If the numbers are small, you can visually scan the values. If they are larger, you can use pattern frequencies to see if the values look the same or within a standard pattern.

You can compare the values to reference tables, or you can create a valid domain set of values. You can import or type the valid value set into the software and compare your data to the valid value set. You can look at minimum and maximum values to see if they are within an expectable range.

I need to caution you that the inferred data type will determine the sort sequence. For example, if the data type is a character, it will do an ASCII sort. If the data type is a number, it will do a numerical sort. Therefore, you need to be aware of the data type to determine the sort sequence. This will also affect the minimum and maximum values. If the field was inferred as a character then 100,000 will appear before 900.

Different fields in the data can be quickly compared to a minimum value. ZIP codes should be greater then 00500. Dates should be greater that a certain date. In fact, some applications allow you to set a minimum and maximum for valid dates. If the value is outside of the range, the data type cannot be inferred as a date because the software assumes it is an invalid date. This is a very quick way to find dates outside of the normal range expected by the business analyst.

I was doing some work at a large airfreight company. They have a large fleet of planes that require maintenance. If a maintenance procedure has not been performed on a plane, they enter a date of 01/01/9999 into the record. This way, they can quickly determine if the procedure has not yet been performed. If they entered a null, it would be unclear if the procedure was performed or just not entered into the system.

One technique I use to determine the validity of values is cross-table analysis. I bring a reference table into the project and then run cross-table analysis against the two fields – one from the customer data and one from the reference table. Sometimes I do not limit the columns in the table I plan to run against the reference table, which helps me find fields of data that overlap with reference data not immediately expected to contain these values.

	Left	% Included Right	Right	% Included Left	
15	empinfo.STATE	95.23	Customer.address3	21.27	
14	empinfo2.STATE	100.00	Customer.address3	21.27	
3	orders.cst	98.90	Customer.address3	95.74	
7	StateCode.StateCode	83.87	Customer.address3	55.31	
17	StateCode.StateName	30.76	Customer.address3	21.27	
1	empinfo2.CITY	100.00	empinfo.CITY	96.62	
2	empinfo2.STATE	100.00	empinfo.STATE	95.23	
11	empinfo2.ADDRESS1	40.54	empinfo.STREET	38.65	
8	empinfo2.ZIP	54.30	empinfo.ZIP	51.89	
5	Customer.address1	79.24	orders.caddr1	76.81	
4	Customer.address2	88.20	orders.ccity	87.43	
13	empinfo.STATE	95.23	orders.cst	21.97	
12	empinfo2.STATE	100.00	orders.cst	21.97	
6	StateCode.StateCode	83.87	orders.cst	57.14	
16	StateCode.StateName	30.76	orders.cst	21.97	
18	Customer.address4	34.90	orders.czip	14.18	

Value	StateCod...	Customer....	Alias		Value	StateCod...	Customer....
BE		4	1		AA		1
BOSTON		1	1				
CA·92121		1	1				
CALIFORNIA		9	1				
COLORADO		1	1				
CONNECTICUT		13	1				
COVE		1	1				
DC·20036		3	1				
FLORIDA		3	1				
FORT·WORTH		1	1				
FT.·LAUDE...		1	1				
GEORGIA		2	1				
HOUSTON		2	1				
ILLINOIS		32	1				
JP		1	1				
KANSAS		1	1				
LOUSIANA		1	1				
MARYLAND		2	1				
MASS		7	1				
MASSACHUS...		4	1				
ME·DURHAM		1	1				
MICHIGAN		2	1				
MINNESOTA		2	1				
MISSOURI		3	1				

Figure 4.2

In Figure 4.2, you can see the comparison of the ISO state table compared to the address3 field of the customer table. It shows that only 48.93 percent of the customer data is contained in the reference table. By sorting on the frequencies in the address3 field, you can quickly find the values and the frequencies that are not contained in the reference data. You can see that address3 contains state and ZIP codes, country codes, and state names instead of codes.

The difference between the two techniques is that validating against a valid value set returns the rows with invalid values.

Validating against a reference table returns the values and frequencies that are not in the reference table.

Nulls

A null has been described as "a special value" in computer programming. Special is right. A null is also one of my most hated values. What does a null value mean to the business? Is it missing, unknown, empty, blank, not applicable, or unavailable? Did the customer refuse to enter a value? Does it mean no or yes? I recently profiled some data, and within the same table one field defined null as a Y while another field defined null as a N.

The problem is that most applications know what a null means only within the context of that application. But now you want to repurpose the data. If you query on a field that is yes or no, you need to replace the null value with something so that subsequent queries to the data return a correct answer. If you have too many nulls in the data, the field may become useless to the new application unless you can replace it with a correct entry that has business value. If there are reasons you have a null–for example, the customer refused to provide an answer–then add that code to the valid value set.

Nulls can create another problem when you try to eliminate duplicate entries in your database. Most deduplicating software creates groups of records to speed up the matching process. If the field that you are grouping contains a null, that record is moved to an incorrect group and is never matched against other records placed in other groups.

Most profiling tools automatically tell you the number and percentage of nulls that exist in each column. This accelerates your analysis, because you need to know if nulls are okay, or if you need to investigate further. My personal preference is that there should never be a null anywhere in the data. If the field is not applicable, then enter "not applicable" in the field. If the record is for a grammar school student and the field is "driver's license," then enter "N/A." If the customer is asked for data that he or she did not have at the time, then enter "unavailable." If the customer does not want to give you their income level, then enter "refused to answer." This way, the information is correct and self-documenting. A null leaves too much unanswered.

Frequency Distributions

Frequency distributions are used in a number of ways. When you look at the frequency distributions of the values, do they look appropriate for the data? If you are mainly a west coast operation, are the frequency distributions correct? Are most of your sales in California, Oregon, and Washington? If you are a women's college, are most of you students female?

Value	Frequency	Percent
MONDAY, JULY 31, 2000	5898	29.48%
SUNDAY, DECEMBER 27, 1998	2792	13.95%
THURSDAY, JANUARY 07, 1999	1405	7.02%
SATURDAY, MARCH 20, 1999	1357	6.78%
WEDNESDAY, APRIL 07, 1999	813	4.06%
FRIDAY, DECEMBER 01, 2000	403	2.01%
WEDNESDAY, DECEMBER 06, 2000	379	1.89%
TUESDAY, SEPTEMBER 14, 1999	292	1.45%
TUESDAY, NOVEMBER 21, 2000	271	1.35%
TUESDAY, NOVEMBER 07, 2000	251	1.25%
FRIDAY, APRIL 23, 1999	155	0.77%
FRIDAY, JANUARY 15, 1999	134	0.66%
MONDAY, APRIL 17, 2000	131	0.65%
FRIDAY, JANUARY 05, 2001	92	0.45%
FRIDAY, AUGUST 04, 2000	86	0.42%
THURSDAY, AUGUST 31, 2000	86	0.42%
WEDNESDAY, DECEMBER 27, 2000	84	0.41%
FRIDAY, NOVEMBER 03, 2000	81	0.40%
MONDAY, DECEMBER 13, 1999	76	0.37%
SATURDAY, APRIL 01, 2000	70	0.34%
WEDNESDAY, DECEMBER 20, 2000	69	0.34%
THURSDAY, JULY 01, 1999	68	0.33%
THURSDAY, DECEMBER 28, 2000	67	0.33%
THURSDAY, JUNE 10, 1999	65	0.32%
SATURDAY, DECEMBER 30, 2000	63	0.31%
FRIDAY, APRIL 02, 1999	62	0.30%
MONDAY, NOVEMBER 27, 2000	61	0.30%
TUESDAY, MARCH 07, 2000	59	0.29%
WEDNESDAY, OCTOBER 04, 2000	59	0.29%
MONDAY, NOVEMBER 06, 2000	58	0.28%
FRIDAY, JUNE 30, 2000	57	0.28%
THURSDAY, APRIL 06, 2000	56	0.27%
WEDNESDAY, SEPTEMBER 06, 2000	55	0.27%
MONDAY, AUGUST 06, 2001	52	0.25%
MONDAY, OCTOBER 25, 1999	52	0.25%
MONDAY, JULY 30, 2001	50	0.24%
TUESDAY, DECEMBER 05, 2000	50	0.24%
WEDNESDAY, JUNE 27, 2001	49	0.24%
SATURDAY, JUNE 30, 2001	48	0.23%
WEDNESDAY, SEPTEMBER 29, 1999	47	0.23%
TUESDAY, FEBRUARY 08, 2000	46	0.22%

Figure 4.3

In Figure 4.3, you see the frequency distribution of different dates. I wonder why many values are July 31. I also question the Saturday and Sunday dates, since this is financial data and the markets are closed on Saturday and Sunday.

I sort on the frequency column all the time. I like to use the top and bottom ten most frequent and least frequent values to find outliers. A very high frequency for one value may be the default value coded into the application for a field, or it may be the first value in a drop-down menu. When an insurance company found a very high instance of broken arms, broken arms turned out to be the first value in a drop-down menu. When an insurance company found a very high instance of broken arms, broken arms turned out to be the first value in a drop-down menu.

Sometimes a value is automatically generated if nothing is entered. Other times, you see a number that is obviously wrong but entered by the agent because a value is required. You see dates like 01/01/01 or values like 99999 or 11111. The data entry person might enter his or her own Social Security number just to get by the field.

Remember the airfreight company mentioned earlier? This company tries to track parts back to the manufacturer. However, some of the systems are older and cannot capture that data. When moving the data to a data warehouse, the company decided to enter a value of 999909999 into the field for all records coming out of the older systems. Some agents found out about this default value and started entering it into the more recent systems, invalidating the information.

Here's another example. In the supermarket, barcode stickers are placed (and soon to be laser etched) on produce because checkout clerks don't know (or are too lazy to look up) the proper Universal Product Code (UPC) for all the different types of produce. Instead, they enter the default value for unknown produce and the correct (we hope) price. Most supermarkets had no clue as to the type or amount produce they actually sell versus the produce that is trashed because it is overripe.

You can also find potentially bad data by looking at the bottom values in the frequency distribution. For example, if you have twenty values with a relatively even distribution, but you find a couple of values with only a few occurrences, this may indicate a problem. Later on, we will discuss applying graphics to view clustering of values.

Pattern Matching

Pattern matching is very useful in identifying several potential issues. You may want to use pattern matching if you want to see if the data needs to be transformed into a standard structure while you are moving it. For example, let's say you are looking at a phone number and you see the following patterns:

9(10)	10 numerical values
9(7)	7 numerical values
9-999-U(7)	A numeric, a dash, 3 numerical values, a dash, and 7 upper case characters
(999)b999-9999	Open parenthesis, 3 numerical values, closed parenthesis, a space, 3 numerical values, a dash, and finally 4 numerical values

These patterns indicate that you have a phone number stored in different formats and that you have seven and ten digit phone numbers. How are you going to handle this?

What if you identify patterns that do not look like valid phone numbers?

For example:
- 9(8)
- 999b9(6)
- 9(6)

Such patterns quickly point out issues.

Pattern matching is great for looking at columns that have a large number of distinct values. For example, look at the following values for an account number:

- U9(7)
- U999U999
- U9(5)U9
- U9(5)UU
- 9(8)
- U9(6)U

As you can see, all the values fit a CHAR 8 data type. If there are two million rows, it would be very difficult to visually inspect them, and you would be hard pressed to write a validation rule unless you know the specific pattern ahead of time.

Latter on, we will look at pattern matching as one technique for validating specific types of data like Social Security numbers Do they look like 999-99-9999 or 9(9)?

Top 10 / Bottom 10

The frequencies top and bottom values are not the only set of top and bottom values you need to view. I also look at sorting the actual values to identify alpha or special characters in a numeric field, as illustrated in Table 4.1. Clearly, this inferred data type would also show you have a problem, but this will give you a better idea how bad the problem is.

Value	Frequency	Percent
Null	1	0.01
07050001	2	0.01
A0560004	12	0.02

Table 4.1

Sorting a date field will show you invalid values like a 01/01/01 or years of 9999. Sorting on numeric fields will show you very low values or very high values. Sorting on money fields will quickly point out negative numbers.

As discussed earlier, you can also use pattern matching to assist you in pointing out anomalies. You can also sort on the pattern frequencies to help identify issues.

Empty Fields

Empty fields are slightly different from null fields. These fields contain blanks or zeros for numeric fields. However, just like nulls, every time I see an empty field I wonder, what does it mean? Do these empty fields mean:

- No value?
- Unavailable?
- Not applicable?
- Not classified?
- Unknown?

On the other hand, empty fields may indicate that we are looking at data from an enterprise application that was never intended to be populated. A few financial services companies have a goal to have no fields empty for their high net worth customers. They profile their gold customers separately and have agents try to track down the information not contained in the record.

Cardinality and Uniqueness

In mathematics, the cardinality of a set is a measure of the "number of elements of the set." In profiling, I look at cardinality as the total number of different or distinct values that exist in a column. Uniqueness is the other value that goes hand in hand with cardinality. Uniqueness is the cardinality divided by the total number of records. This value usually shows up as the percent unique column in the software. Cardinality is important because the higher the number, the longer it will take the software to pro-file the column, and it is a major component of uniqueness.

Uniqueness is important in understanding some values. When I am looking for a key, I sort on the percent unique column and start looking at the percentages. Is there a column that is 100-percent unique? We will discuss this further when we get to key analysis.

Ranges

Ranges help identify anomalies by finding a high concentra-tion of values in ranges thought to have a more even distribution of values. For example, you would expect to see the field of salary ranges as an even distribution of values until you get to the ex-ecutive level.

Reviewing ranges might show data that is actually two types of data. When you look at salary ranges and see two distinct clusters of the data, you might be looking at hourly and yearly values.

Later, we will discuss the segmenting of the data. Ranges in the segmentation frequently reveal anomalies.

Aggregations

Aggregations show up in two different ways during profiling. First, there are possible aggregations that exist within the record. For example, you may have the fields, "quantity times unit cost equals total amount." When you run table analysis, you had better find a two-column determinate – quantity and unit cost – which has total amount as a dependent. If you do not find that two-column determinate, somewhere, someone changed the formula.

Second, aggregations show up when you are trying to determine the extent of the cost of a data anomaly. Here's an example. One company wanted to know what its data quality issue was with respect to real dollars. The problem was that this company had invalid account types in its data. The company wanted to view the total order amounts by bad account type to see if this was a major or minor issue with regard to its actual customer orders.

Another example of using aggregations to validate data is to add up total deposits by date and compare it to the deposit records to see if items were missed in creating the deposits or if records were missing, based on deposits being greater then the aggregations. I am sure you can think of ways to use aggregations to validate your data or further define the cost of the bad data.

Visual Inspection

Visual inspection is just that: looking at all the distinct values in a column. When there are relatively small numbers of values, it is easy to look and see if something looks funny.

Table 4.2 shows a small set of values.

Value	Frequency	Percent
FRAGRANCE·JUICES	141	1.37
FACIAL·CARE	52	0.50
NAIL·COLOR	33	0.32
HAND·&·BODY·CARE	30	0.29
BATH·&·SHOWER	26	0.25
EYE·COLOR	4	0.03
LIP·COLOR	4	0.03
LIPCOLOR	4	0.03

Table 4.2

You do not need to look very long to find that the term "lip color" is spelled as both one word and two. You can usually identify these types of anomalies quickly. If there is a high cardinality of the values, I tend to just hold the mouse to the scroll bar and let the values fly by. If there are some strange values in the column, they sometimes jump out at you. In addition, I sort the values and look for different spellings or upper and lower case values within the same column. Pattern analysis help find these issues as well, but visual inspection is also important.

Consecutive Numbers

Consecutive numbers show up in columns like check numbers or automatically generated keys. Sometimes it is important to know if there are missing sequential values in check numbers. Personally, I do not write out many checks, and my bank check database is small enough that I can scan the numbers and see if

I am missing any values. But what if you write a million checks a month? How can you find out if you are missing any values?

The quickest way I know is to look at the minimum value, subtract that from the maximum value, add one, and compare that to the number of distinct values. They should be equal. Look at the values 1, 2, 3, and 4. Subtract 1 from 4 add 1 and you get 4 values.

Before you do this, you should look at percent distinct. If the values are not distinct, you cannot have consecutive values. You should also look at the data type, length, and pattern to make sure all the values look the same. Otherwise, doing the calculations is a waste of time.

Data Structure

Data profiling software helps you understand or validate the data structure of a table or a set of tables. Table analysis yields the determinants and dependents. Using table analysis, you can validate the relationships that exist within the data. Some software tools have additional steps that allow you to automatically find inferred keys and inferred subtables. I like to let the software do the initial validation of the keys.

Another note of caution. None of the profiling tools I have used executes table analysis against the full population of the data. The tools do it against a statistical sample of the data. The good thing is if a relationship does not exist in the sample, it does not exist in the full population of the data. The bad thing is if the relationship exits in the sample, it may not exit in the full population.

The advantage of some profiling tools is that they allow you to quickly and easily validate your findings against the full population of the data. For a single table, you simply right click on what you have defined as the key and select validate. The software runs against the full population and shows any violations. You can also build alternate keys and validate these. I use the validate alternate keys function to validate natural keys. For example, there might be an employee ID as the key to the table. But there is also the Social Security number in the table, and that should also be unique.

I have started using the validate alternate keys function to look for duplicate records in the table. I build a key that includes first name, last name, suffix, city, and state. This shows me any exact matches to these fields by showing violations. Unlike most data quality software matching algorithms that allow you to use fuzzy matching technologies, these are exact matches only.

I have also used the validate alternate keys function to see if there are violations in the combination of two fields. For example, let's say I want to test to see if there are violations in country and currency code. If the country is USA, then the currency code should be USD. I build an alternate key, which includes the two columns. The software shows me the frequencies of the two field combinations. I can then sort on either field to see if there is more than one country–currency combination. In the next section, we will look at the structure of multiple tables.

Global Product Classification (GPC)

The global standards management process was created to build and maintain solutions that meet the needs of the members in the supply chain. Global product classification is facilitated by the Global Commerce Initiative (GCI), a global user group comprised of the world's biggest multinational manufacturers and retailers, owned by EAN International (GS1) and hosted and managed by ACNielsen as the service provider to the industry.

EAN.UCC global product classification provides both manufacturers and retailers with a global standard for classifying product information. This standard gives trading partners access to a common language for grouping products alongside their own internal or external classification frameworks.

Global product classification allows trading partners to communicate more efficiently and accurately throughout their supply chain activities and is a key enabler to the data synchronization process.

Here is a product classification example. I picked the music industry.

Segment code 61000000 music
- Family code 61010000 musical instruments/accessories
- - Class 61010200 musical instruments (nonpowered)
- - - Core attribute type 20000820 brass wind musical instrument (nonpowered)

- - - - Core attribute value

30007094	CORNET
30007095	DOUBLE HORN
30007096	EUPHONIUM
30007097	FLUGEL HORN
30007098	FRENCH HORN
30010843	SAXOPHONE
30007099	SOUSAPHONE
30007100	TROMBONE
30007101	TRUMPET
30007102	TUBA
30002515	UNCLASSIFIED
30002518	UNIDENTIFIED

As you can see, classification is a hierarchical structure of codes used to identify a product. This particular structure starts with music as the main category, moves to musical instruments, further breaks down into nonpowered, continues to brass wind nonpowered instruments, then finally identifies the actual instruments. Determining the breakdown of a classification structure poses a significant challenge to many companies. Depending on how the data is stored, you could have three fields that, when combined, point to one value. This means that the code, attribute type, and attribute value point to one and only one attribute description.

To validate the structure, I recommend building an alternate key consisting of the code, attribute type, and attribute value and test that structure. Any violations of the key are potential break-downs in the classification structure.

Cross-Table Analysis

There are many examples of cross-table analysis delivering business value. After completing the month end book closing, one company found that its debits did not equal its credits. This discrepancy showed up when the data between the two fields–the debit and the credit fields–turned out not to be 100 percent redundant.

Another company found that less than 100 percent redundancy between the fields for shipping tickets and billing invoices. By performing cross-table analysis, this company identified millions of dollars of product that was shipped but was never billed to the customer.

How does cross-table analysis work? Earlier in this book, I mentioned that in the column profiling step, the software builds a distinct value set for every column in the table. Cross-table profiling uses the distinct value set that exists for each column and compares it to all the other distinct value sets in the project. It shows the percentage of overlap that exists between the data in the column pairs. It shows the results as column pairs with a percentage of values that exist in one table that are also contained in another distinct value set. Depending on the number of tables, columns, and distinct values, cross-table analysis may take a while. However, going back to my data warehouse days, does it matter how long a task takes if you get an actionable answer? The same is true here. If I find data integrity or invalid values that can negatively affect the business, does it really matter that it a computer running has to run full out for two hours to give me this valuable information?

An example of cross-table analysis is in Figure 4.4.

	Left	% Included Right	Right	% Included Left
1	empinfo.DEPTNM	100.00	empinfo2.DEPTNAME	100.00
2	Product.pd_name	100.00	orders.desc	100.00
3	orders.cst	100.00	orders.STGLOC	100.00
4	Product.price	100.00	orders.c_u	99.45
5	empinfo2.CITY	100.00	empinfo.CITY	96.62
6	empinfo2.STATE	100.00	empinfo.STATE	95.23
7	orders.cst	98.90	Customer.address3	95.74
8	orders.STGLOC	98.90	Customer.address3	95.74
9	Product.brand	100.00	orders.Brand	93.75
10	empinfo2.JOBTITLE	99.03	empinfo.TITLE	94.49
11	empinfo2.L_NAME	99.54	empinfo.L_NAME	93.99
12	empinfo2.F_NAME	100.00	empinfo.F_NAME	92.67
13	orders.CNTYGLOC	99.95	Customer.zip_or_postcode	87.74
14	orders.CTYGLOC	99.90	Customer.address2	87.56
15	orders.CTYGLOC	100.00	orders.ccity	86.87
16	orders.NGLOC	99.93	Customer.company_name	82.85
17	orders.A1GLOC	99.93	Customer.address1	79.18
18	Customer.address2	88.20	orders.ccity	87.43
19	orders.CGLOC	99.97	Customer.cust_number	77.95
20	orders.A1GLOC	99.95	orders.caddr1	76.76
21	Customer.contact_name	82.23	orders.cname	81.07
22	Customer.address1	79.24	orders.caddr1	76.81
23	orders.item	81.81	orders.qty	69.23
24	empinfo2.GENDER	80.00	empinfo.GENDER	66.66
25	orders.clocid	100.00	orders.item	54.54
26	StateCode.StateCode	83.87	orders.cst	57.14
27	StateCode.StateCode	83.87	orders.STGLOC	57.14
28	StateCode.StateCode	83.87	Customer.address3	55.31
29	orders.prod id	100.00	Product.product_id	47.46
30	orders.clocid	100.00	orders.qty	46.15
31	empinfo2.ZIP	54.30	empinfo.ZIP	51.89

E Source.Inferred Redundancies

V...	StateCod...	Customer....	Ali
AA	1		
AE	4		
AK	1	12	
AL	1	21	
AP	1		
AR	1	21	
AS	1		
AZ	1	76	
PP		4	

Value	StateCod...	Customer....
AA	1	

Figure 4.4

In this example, you see 100 percent of the values in the pd_ name field from the product table are contained in the description field from the order table, and 100 percent of the values in the description field from the order table are contained in the pd_name field from the product table. In the highlighted field, you see that the reference table for state code has a 83.87 percent overlap with address3 field in the customer table. This just means you are not doing business in 16 percent of the States. However, there is only a 55.31 percent overlap of the values in the address3 field in the customer table with the state code table. That usually means that your data is bad (or your reference data needs to be updated). If you look at the actual values, you notice that many of the values contain the state spelled out versus using the two-character state code.

I am usually looking for primary–foreign key relationships that should exist with in the data. If I do not find these relationships, then one of two things may have happened: the relationship does not exist in the data, or there are too many distinct values in the two columns. Coincidentally, they did not overlap in the same area. Later in the book, we will discuss validating relationships and the techniques to do this.

In performing cross-table analysis, some of the business issues I am looking for include:

- Are there values in the order table that are not in the product table?
- Are there sales people in the commission system who are not in the employee table?
- Are there customers of the bank that are on the government watch list?
- Are there states or country codes that do not exist?
- Are there airports that we land at that we are not legally entitled to use?

I also use cross-table analysis to look for values that are not in a reference table. I import the table just like any other table that I am profiling. Let us say I have an ISO state table used in the earlier example. I run cross-table analysis using the state reference table and all the address data I have in the project. I should see 100 percent overlap. As this example illustrates, it is very easy to pick out the invalid values.

Data Segmentation

The first time I profile data, I do the entire table and every column in the table. I want to find overall results. As I learn more and more about the business and its data, I may want to look at subsets of the data.

Once I profile the entire population of the data, I may want to segment the data for different reasons. These reasons are usually to identify expected differences (or to find unexpected differences) in the structure or quality of the data.

Regional Differences

Regional differences show up in different industries for different reasons. The insurance industry has different laws depending on the state in which they are offering different products. The laws covering auto insurance differ state by state. Therefore, profiling data segmented by state helps identify potential liabilities with the data for each state. Certain states require data to be kept on customers that are not required by other states. Profiling data state-by-state can help identify fields that are required in New Jersey that are not required to be gathered in California. I find that the structure of the data when profiled state-by-state is sometimes different than the data profiled as a whole.

Companies with major international operations have different requirements than companies that mainly do business in North America. A few simple fields like phone number, postal code, address, and even names will differ greatly from one country to another. Again, I expect the structure of the data would vary slightly, country by country.

Cable companies, by the nature of how they were required to be approved on a town-by-town, state-by-state basis, also show differences in their customer segmentation. In addition, the way these companies traded cable operations over the years also show differences based on the different systems they used for provisioning the customers over time. In addition, many cell phone companies were individual businesses operating under one name for a long time.

The entire communications industry shows differences in its data on a regional or state-by-state basis. These regional differences exist because local phone businesses were separated from long distance businesses. Then both businesses acquired or built their own cable and wireless businesses before deregulation enabled them to bring all their businesses together. So, depending on at what point the customer was acquired, there will be different qualities in the data. I expect the local phone customer to have excellent phone numbers and address information but have issues with its the wireless or cable data.

Other industries have similar differences in segmentation based upon regional differences. It is important to be aware of these before you begin profiling the data.

Pay Grade

Pay grade is another way to segment the data. You can look at the structure and quality of your data based upon pay grade. Do you want to look at the executive level and realize you do not have the CIO's home phone number on file? What about salary levels? The minimum and maximum for salary will differ greatly by pay grade. If you look at clusters of salary based upon pay grade, you see outliers very quickly. You can identify if someone is being overpaid (or underpaid like me). I mentioned before that you also need to be sure you are comparing apples to apples. Are you looking at exempt and nonexempt employees in the same pay grade, i.e., salaried vs. hourly? Are there benefits that are offered to some pay grades that are not offered to others?

Differences Over Time

For different reasons, values change over time. Unit costs, for example, tend to trend up over time. Let's look at another example: salary. Rumor has it that salaries increase over time. While I have never experienced this phenomenon, maybe you have. Other values, like auto or home loan amounts and durations, have definitely increased over time. Remember when a car loan was up to three years and home loans were for only thirty years? These are reasons why you may want to profile segments of data based on time.

Another reason is that the database may have been modified, and you may want to see the relationships that existed before and after a change in the database. I have seen contents of a field in a database change over time. A few examples immediately jump to mind:

- A company started saving Social Security information in a field that used to be used to store fishing license numbers.
- Another company started storing Internet passwords in a Child_5_name field.
- How many of you have not seen data in filler fields?

For these reasons, you may want to profile segments of the database after you have profiled the entire population of the database. Doing so may show relationships that did not exist in the entire population that now show up in the newer segments.

Differences by Customer Type

I am seeing a trend in which financial institutions are segmenting their customer data by customer type. Let's look at an example of this trend.

Let's say a retail investment services company has different levels of customers – customers who have investments accounts valued at zero to 100,000 dollars, 100,000 to 500,000, 500,000 to one million dollars, one million to 20 million dollars, and above 20 million dollars. The company profiles each customer segment separately. If a single null value in any field appeared for the above 20 million dollar level, the company immediately researched the information and entered it into their system. Conversely, the information for the customer at the zero to 100,000 dollar level is not a major concern. Certain information, like a tax ID, is vitally important for all customers, but if a phone number for the zero to 100,000 dollar customer is missing, that is perceived as an inconvenience.

Similarly, an airline can segment its data based on silver, gold, and platinum customer levels. When running profiling for companies that segment their customers like this, you are much more interested in the null rule and empty field analysis. I doubt that differences in structure will show up like the other types of segmentation.

These are just some of the reasons you may want to segment and profile the data segment after you have profiled all of the data. It is important to see what the structure looks like for all of the data before you begin segmenting the data. As you profile all of the data, you may begin to see holes in the data. Remember: what you see in profiling the data is important, but what you don't see is just as important. What you were expecting to see and did not may be because you may need to segment the data, or the relationship you were expecting to find did not show up because of issues in the data.

Hidden Business Rules

Here's a question: do you have all your original application developers on staff? Do you have any? I have seen companies scared silly about turning off an application that's supposedly at the core of the business, but no one knows what it does. When I profile data from applications, I find relationships in the data that no one knew existed. These relationships are usually enforced by the application. Of course, there is no documentation detailing these rules, and the developers have long since retired.

Profiling data will bring these rules out. Sometimes the rules found in the data are coincidences, but other times they are long-buried business rules that, if you search long enough, you will find an old timer who can tell you if they still need to be enforced. The problem is when you move the data, you need to understand and enforce these rules in the new application.

Embedded Tables

Most systems denormalize data for many good reasons: ease of reporting, performance, etc. Most old mainframe systems were never normalized. When profiling the data and doing table analysis, there are three main outcomes: 1) individual determinant–dependent references; 2) key analysis; and 3) subtable analysis. I should back up here and explain that one of the outputs of a data profiling tool may be a third normal form of the tables in the project. Table analysis quickly helps you identify subtables that can be broken out into their own tables.

In the example in Figure 4.5, a salesperson's first name, last name, and title are imbedded in an order file. There is no reason (except the normal reasons for denormalizing data) that this could not be in an employee or salesperson table. Profiling software finds these imbedded tables automatically.

	Determinants	Dependent	Validation
	E Source.orders.orders_#1.Inferred Dependencies		
33	cname	Brand	True
34	caddr1	A1GLOC	True
35	caddr1	clocid	True
36	caddr1	cphone	True
37	ccity	CTYGLOC	Gray
38	ccity	clocid	Gray
39	ccity	cphone	True
40	czip	ZIPGLOC	True
41	czip	cphone	True
42	paycode	cphone	True
43	paycode	method	True
44	paycode	terms	True
45	method	cphone	True
46	method	terms	True
47	terms	cphone	Gray
48	sales id	cphone	True
49	sales id	last	True
50	sales id	first	True
51	sales id	title	True
52	last	cphone	True
53	first	cphone	True
54	title	cphone	Gray
55	order date	cphone	Gray
56	ship code	cphone	True
57	ship code	ship desc	True
58	ship desc	cphone	True
59	ship desc	ship code	True
60	prod id	desc	True
61	prod id	cphone	True
62	prod id	item	Gray
63	prod id	Brand	True

Figure 4.5

Derived Value Columns

Derived or calculated columns are columns that are or should be dependent on other fields in the table. A simple example is total cost. This field is dependent on quantity and unit cost. This relationship shows up in table analysis. A combined determinant of unit cost and quantity points to the dependent of total cost. If it does not, then someone changed the formula over time. Remember, it is not only important what the software shows you; it is also important what it does not show you.

Noise

Noise is something I look for every time I profile data. Noise are values like N/A, none, null, ?, ???, ?????, unknown, 99999, 11111, 0 or multiple blanks, do not use, system test, do not call, do not mail. And the list goes on and on. As I profile the data, I usually find additional values. Luckily, the software I use has the feature called autotags. These are business rules that automatically run against every field in the column profiling process.

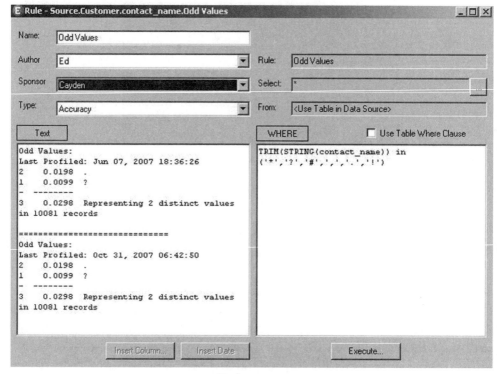

Figure 4.6

The three autotags I use all the time are: 1) constant data; 2) special characters; and 3) missing data. The constant data rule looks for fields that have only one value or one value and nulls. This field is a constant. Constant fields are not used; therefore, I need not spend time on them and only identify them to the ETL developer as fields he can ignore. Since they are constant, they also do not need to be moved.

The special characters autotags are configured to look for values like: ?, *, !, ( ), etc. These values usually are not expected in the data, and this rule helps me identify fields that will require special attention, especially by the ETL developer. Most likely, they will need to be stripped from the data when it is repurposed. Figure 4.6 shows an example of the special characters rule.

The missing data autotags are fields that have blanks, null, N/A, none, do not use, not applicable, etc. Again, these fields need special attention to determine if they are also unused or if the records containing these values are bad.

The nice feature inherent in autotags is that they are configurable. I was profiling a company's mainframe data and, since the mainframe has no concept of nulls, they included "*No Data" in all fields for which it did not have a value. I quickly modified the autotag and had it look for missing data, which now included "*No Data".

Multiuse (Overloaded) Fields

Multiuse or overloaded fields are fields with more than one business fact in the field. These are different from free form text fields in that they were originally designed for one fact. Over the years, customer service agents needed to add an additional and related fact, but the application did not allow it. Therefore, they stuffed the additional data into the one field.

Two examples of multiuse or overloaded fields are: 1) a field that contains a date and sometimes a number; and 2) a field that contains a certification and a date. The first one is a delivery date and the number is a code describing delivery day options, such as Monday through Friday, Monday through Saturday, weekends only, a single day of the week, etc. The second one is a medical certification and the date it was achieved.

In the first example, the field was intended only to hold the delivery date. Sometime after the system was placed in operation, the shipping department also needed to know about delivery options for the customer in case the delivery needed to be rescheduled. The second example was intended to capture a certification. Later, it became important to capture the date it was attained.

Multiuse fields are easy to diagnose. I find them by first looking at the data types. In the first example, I expect to see a date data type. This one almost jumps off the screen at you. If you do not see it immediately, looking at the patterns clinches it.

The second example is not as intuitive. Since you expect character data, the dates after the certification shows up only by looking at the value frequencies and doing a visual inspection. If you know the maximum length of the certifications (e.g., MBA or BBA), you look for a three-character alpha field. If the data type is wrong, it shows up there, or patterns also show it.

Cross Field Analysis

Cross-field analysis is the concept of using one or more fields to validate another field. Let us look at a simple example in Table 4.3:

Title	Pay Grade	Salary Range	Department
Sales Engineer	5 or 6	2,000 – 8,000	Sales
Senior Sales Engineer	7 or 8	7,000 – 15,000	Sales
Principal Sales Engineer	9 or 10	10,000 – 20,000	Sales
Product Specialist	10 or 11	15,000 – 25,000	Sales

Table 4.3

Here we see four fields that can be used to validate one another. I can use title to build a business rule to confirm that the pay grade and salary ranges are correct. I can also use the pay grade to build a business rule to validate the salary ranges. When you use cross-field analysis to build business rules, you need to be aware that usually there are no hard and fast rules. Many business rules are more general in nature, and there are exceptions to the rules. For example, while my title is Product Specialist, I am still in pay grade 5, and my salary range is below the range for a pay grade of five. However, when drilling down to show the exceptions to this rule, someone would notice it was me and immediately validate this exception as allowable.

Cross-field analysis is also useful for banks, which have fields like loan type, length of loan, interest rate, and collateral. I used this example before when discussing business rules. You can use the loan type to validate the loan length range and the interest rate range.

I can use the fields customer type, invoice amount, status, credit limit to validate the invoice amount, and credit limit using customer type. I can also use the status field to determine if the other fields are appropriate.

Cross-field analysis is very powerful, but you need to understand the data and have a thorough knowledge of the business. You also need to know when the rules are hard and fast and when you need to allow exceptions.

Referential Integrity

Referential integrity in a relational database is defined as consistency between coupled tables. Referential integrity is usually enforced by the combination of a primary key or candidate key and a foreign key. For referential integrity to hold, any field in a table that is declared a foreign key can contain only values from a parent table's primary key or a candidate key. For instance, deleting a record that contains a value referred to by a foreign key in another table would break referential integrity. The RDBMS enforces referential integrity, normally either by deleting the foreign key rows as well to maintain integrity, or by returning an error and not performing the delete. The method used is be defined in the definition of the referential integrity constraint.

One example of referential integrity is a product sold that is not in the product table. Let's say this product has been discontinued, but you need to validate that. I have found examples of products that were shipped but never billed, identifying millions of unrecovered dollars for one company. Other examples include line items for an invoice but no invoice header record, or commissions paid to a salesperson who is not in the employee file. Was this salesperson just terminated, and these are commissions due from last quarter?

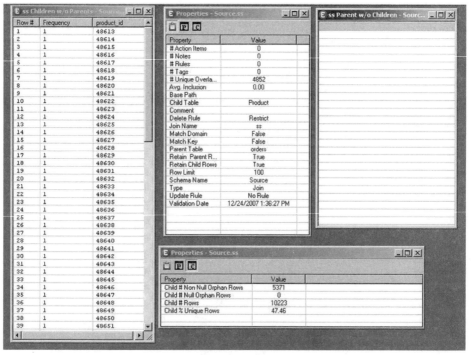

Figure 4.7

The technique used to find these issues is sometimes called orphan analysis. You can perform orphan analysis by validating the structure of each table, identifying the keys for each, by using a feature called profile foreign keys. This feature takes the primary keys defined for each table and looks in the valid value sets for all of the columns to find any overlap. Once you find the suspect relationships, you right click and validate your findings. This shows any orphans.

You can also perform orphan analysis by using the validating joins feature. As discussed earlier, I build a join between the sales tracking system and the product table. There should be a relationship between the product ID in the sales system and the product ID in the product table. I then look for orphans between the two tables.

In Figure 4.7, you see that in the upper left hand corner there are 5,371 orphan rows. These products are not in the order file. While this is a problem with the business not selling these products, it is not a data issue (although the product managers of those products would not like the answer). In the lower left hand column, you notice there are no orphan rows. This means you are not selling anything that is not in the product table. Therefore, that is a good thing for the business, not selling things that are not in the product table (although I have worked with some salespeople that did this occasionally).

VALIDATION

As I mentioned earlier, table and cross table analysis do not perform against the full population of the data. While both do an excellent job of identifying keys and cross table joins, they are not always valid if the number of distinct values is greater than the maximum number of stored values. That is usually sixteen thousand. This is where the validation capabilities of the software come into play. Some of the software available today makes it very easy to validate your findings. With one tool in particular, it is a simple right click and validate. Let us look at the different validation capabilities.

Key Analysis

Key analysis is a technique of identifying the key to a table. The nice thing about profiling software is it helps identify the primary key and any natural keys. It does this during the single table analysis step. It can automatically determine multiple column keys. The default for some software packages is five columns participating in a key. Some vendors recommend that starting with two or three columns because for every increase in the number of columns, the software will have to do an exponential number of calculations.

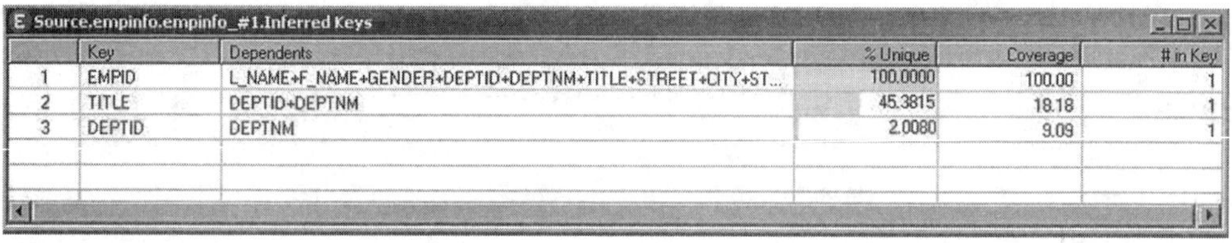

	Key	Dependents	% Unique	Coverage	# in Key
1	EMPID	L_NAME+F_NAME+GENDER+DEPTID+DEPTNM+TITLE+STREET+CITY+ST...	100.0000	100.00	1
2	TITLE	DEPTID+DEPTNM	45.3815	18.18	1
3	DEPTID	DEPTNM	2.0080	9.09	1

E Source.empinfo.empinfo_#1.Inferred Keys

Figure 4.8

The most important thing to remember is that the analysis is performed against the sample data, not the entire file. Key analysis is the technique of validating the findings of table analysis against the full population of the data. In table analysis, the software will suggest possible keys. It can identify multiple possibilities of potential keys. You, as the subject matter expert, must identify which of these possibilities is the actual key. Different vendors have different terminologies for this, but in the end, you must explicitly identify the key to the profiling software.

Figure 4.8 shows a simple example of key analysis. There is only one field that is 100 percent unique and covers 100 percent of the fields. Once you have identified this field, you need to right click and identify it as the key. You can then easily just right click and validate the key against the entire source file. The software then allows you to view any exceptions if they exist.

I can also validate alternate keys. Even if the software does not identify a key or does not validate the key against the sample, I can still validate the key against the entire source by creating an alternate key and validating it. It may turn out that the few issues with the key are easily explainable, and that the key should be what you determined as the alternate key.

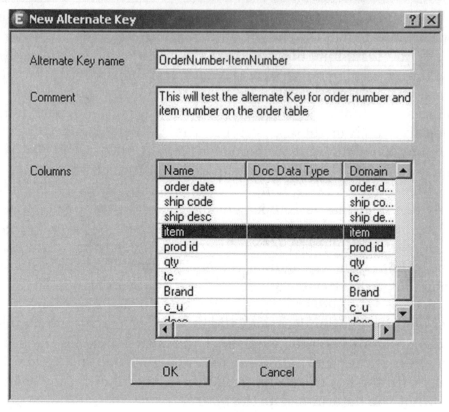

Figure 4.9

Figure 4.9 show the validation step. I have selected both the order number and item number to be validated as the key.

Once you identify keys for each of the tables, you can do primary–foreign keys analysis. Since you identified the primary keys, the software now searches though the tables, looking for redundant data of those identified keys. If it can find redundant fields, it identifies them for you and determines if these are foreign keys or just that the data does not represent the same business fact.

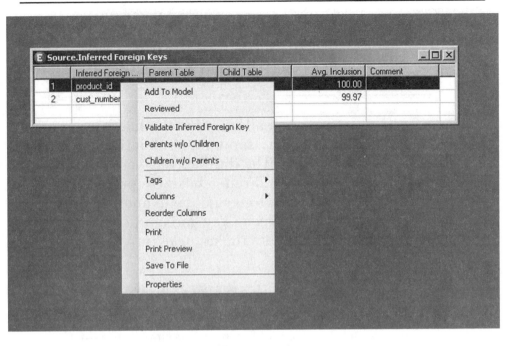

Figure 4.10

In Figure 4.10, you see the inferred foreign keys. Just by right clicking on the Product_ID from the product and custord tables, you can validate that relationship against the full population of the data. If you still have orphans, this may or may not be an issue. In this example, it is be okay to have product values that are not in the order table. This means not every product is currently being sold in the existing orders. However, if you have Product_IDs in the order table that are not in the product table, then you selling products that do not exist in your product table.

On the other hand, if you have a relationship between orders and employee. It is okay to have employees that are not in the orders, but it is not okay to have employees in the orders that are not in the employee table.

While not as important to the DBA, natural keys are important to the business. Earlier we looked at an example using a Social Security number. While it is not a key to the table, you may want to make sure it is a natural key in the data. You can validate natural keys by creating an alternate key and validating it against the source table.

Join Validation

The profiling software also allows you to validate a join. The procedure to validate a join is similar to validating a primary key–foreign key relationship. The difference is you build the relationship and then validate it. From a business prospective, you look for values in one table that may not be in another table. For example, you validate the primary key–foreign key of employee ID, but you may want to validate the natural keys like Social Security numbers.

Validate Values Using Reference Data

One of the primary uses of join validation is to test the values of your data against reference data. If you have reference data, you can build a join and test it to see if you have orphans. Orphans are values that are in your data that are not in the reference data. This is different from testing against valid values in a business rule or drill down. The results of such a business rule test returns the rows that fail the test. This technique only returns the values that are not in the reference data and the frequencies of those that fail. The technique you use depends on the goals of your profiling exercise. If all you need are the invalid values, you should do it this way. If you need to find the actual rows that fail, you should write a business rule or do a drill down.

Vertical Merge Validation

A vertical merge shows you the results of an inner join. An inner join finds the intersection between the two tables. The exceptions for a vertical merge are records that are the same in both tables. The business reason for validating this type of merge is to preempt the combining of two tables that should not have any overlapping values. The best example is bringing together two employee files. Let's say you just bought another company, and you are combining the employee files. You want to check to see if there are common employee IDs or Social Security numbers in the two files.

Duplicates

Finding duplicates from a business prospect is very important. Are all records for customers identified on "credit hold" labeled as such in all of our systems? Any orphans may be potential issues. What about insurance coverage? If you are dropped from coverage, are all the systems in the insurance company updated at the same time? If I upgrade to a new platinum level membership, do all the systems identify me at the proper level? If an employee is terminated, are all the systems updated to reflect this fact?

I use the following technique when I look for duplicate records. I create an alternate key of many fields in the record. I may create an alternate key of first name, last name, street address, city, state, and ZIP code. When I validate this key, any duplicates usually show up as a violation. These violations are exact duplicate records. It also shows the frequencies of the duplicate records if I have more than one.

This is not what data quality programs do when they search for duplicate records. These programs use the concept of fuzzy matching. Fuzzy matching matches two records that have similar address but not the same information. Let's say the last name in one record is Lindsey, and the other last name is Lindsay. This, along with the rest of the match fields, is not an exact match but close enough to where you may consider it a match. The same can be true if there is a transposition error in the ZIP code. Different algorithms are used for different types of data but the result is a near match, which can be considered a match. If you need to do fuzzy matching, profiling is not the tool to use.

TAGS/NOTES

As a feature of profiling software, tags help you document all the issues you find in the data. Some software products have only one type of tag. Others have multiple types of tag. For example, one vendor has notes, action items, business rules, and transformations. Whether you have multiple types of tags or one type, you still perform the same functions, regardless of how many tag types your software provides. You document all the anomalies you find and getting assistance from different members of the team to determine if they are allowable or required to be repaired.

Note Tags

I use note tags for documentation. As I meet with different members of a company, I learn more and more about the data. All that knowledge needs to be collected somewhere. I use a note for every piece of knowledge I learn. Let's say I have a set of codes for a field. As I learn the meaning of the codes, I create a note and attach it to a field. I also put in the top and bottom ten most frequent values so anyone following up the analysis has an idea of what the data in each of the fields looks like from the reports that can be generated.

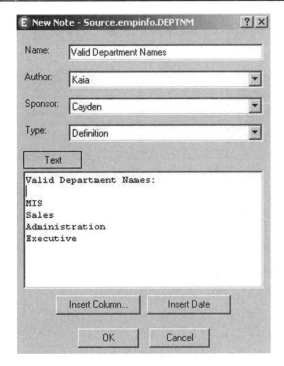

Figure 4.11

In Figure 4.11, you see an example of a note where I identify all the valid department names. Notes are quick and simple but very effective in documenting business knowledge about the fields and tables.

Action Item Tags

As I identify anomalies in the data, I use action item tags to document the issues I encounter. These are different from documentation that I put in the notes. Action item tags are open issues that need to be investigated by members of the team. Figure 4.12 illustrates this point.

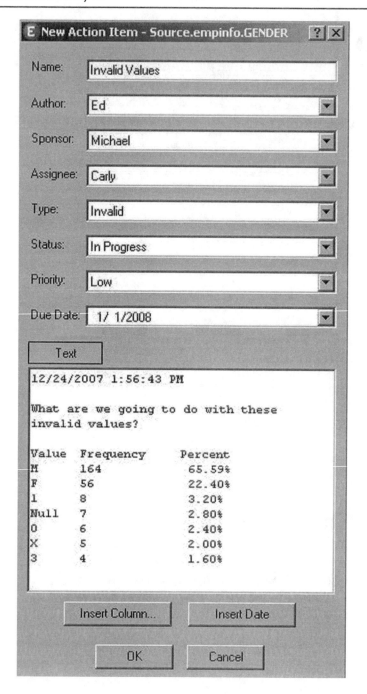

Figure 4.12

Figure 4.12 shows an action tag that identifies a number of issues with an indicator field for gender. Normally, I expect to find two values in a gender field. There are at least two ways this field can be corrected. One is to drill down on each anomaly and try to identify the correct value that should be in the record. Another way is to use a data quality software product that can infer the gender of a person from the first name. This is not something that can accurately identify every occurrence, but it can correct many records. In the earlier example, you have only a small number of records. What if you have millions?

Business Rule Tags

The business rule tags are the executable business rules that run against the source data. These are the different rules that you use to look for anomalies by writing data rules, like comparing two or more fields in the table, to validate relationships. This was discussed previously in cross-field analysis. As a feature of profiling software, business rule tags document and implement this functionality.

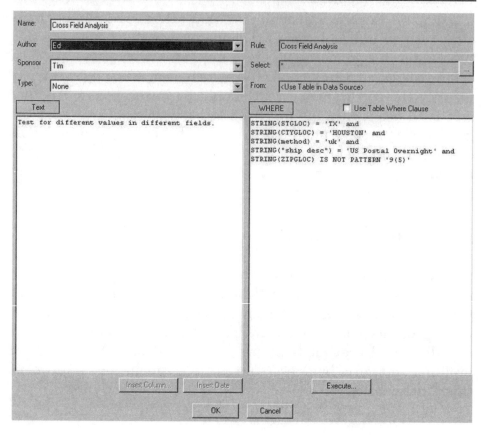

Figure 4.13

In Figure 4.13, you can see this rule tests a number of cross field relationships. Business rules can get quite complex. They are extremely useful when you need to profile the same or similar data on a regular basis. Remember the retail pharmacy company that was moving from multiple systems into one centralized pharmacy system? This company can profile its stores a couple at a time. As the company begins to understand its data, it can develop the business rules to validate their data. Once the company develops the rules, the data profiling project team can then run a complete set of rules against the next set of store extracts. This will produce the records that fail the business rules. The team can then research the failures and correct the business rules based upon the investigation. When finish profiling all of the stores, the team has a complete set of business rules that can be used in the ultimate ETL process when the time comes to move the data from all the stores to the centralized system.

Transformation Rule Tags

Transformation rule tags are used to document all the transformations that need to take place to move the data from one system to the new system, or to cleanse an existing system. These rules might be conversions from a numeric representation to an alpha representation. They might be all the data cleansing and standardization rules the data need to be executed during the ETL process. Therefore, it makes sense to document the ETL rules you need to document in transformation rule tags.

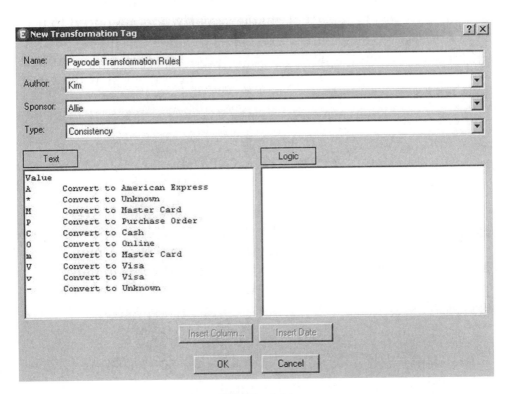

Figure 4.14

As you can see in Figure 4.14, this rule documents how all of the methods of payments need to be converted during the ETL process.

Calculations

Calculations are fields that are calculated using other fields in the record. For example, "Unit cost times quantity equals the calculated field total cost." Other examples include reorder quantity, profit margins, or bonuses. When you run table analysis, this relationship should show up as unit cost, and quantity determines total field. If the software does not find this relationship, you need to investigate further. Did someone change the formula? In the case of bonuses, I am sure it changes yearly. You may need to use a where clause to select records, year by year. You have heard it before, but it bears repeating: It is not only important what the software finds in the data; it is also important what it does not find.

Special Analysis

Sometimes you are interested in only very specific results, so special analysis is required. For example, you may be interested only in those fields that are missing values. Or you may be interested in finding indicator fields, fields that contain only a few values (like Y or N; or M, F, or U). Here are a few examples of special analysis.

Empty Fields

Empty fields are columns whose values include only nulls, blanks, or zeros. This analysis includes columns that contain spaces or null for text data types and null or zeros for numeric data types. These fields usually need to be eliminated during the ETL process. These are different from missing values, which are fields that were never used.

Missing Values

Columns that generally contain values but also have nulls, blanks, or zeros need to be analyzed to determine what the meaning of these missing values. If I have an indicator field but 20 percent of the values are null, what does a null mean? When I was working with a large pharmacy retailer's data, the application put in an indicator of null. The problem was that in one field a null meant an N, while in another field a null meant a Y. This data was being moved to a new application, and the retailer needed to change these values. It needed to happen on a field-by-field basis. New banking regulations prohibit missing values in required fields. For example, you cannot open an account unless you have a physical address.

Constant Fields

Columns that contain fewer than four distinct values are possible constants. Indicator fields fall into this category, but they are usually easy to spot. When you look at the frequency values of constant fields, they are usually 90 to 95 percent one value, with a few other values at very low frequencies. Technically, a constant field contains only one value, but sometimes there are a few bad values as well, and this analysis helps ferret them out. These fields may need to be eliminated during the ETL process.

Inferred Data Type Analysis

Some companies want to see when the inferred data type does not match the documented data type. Sometimes this is by design. A phone number field is set up as a character field, but the software infers it to be a number. ZIP code is another example. While it is a number, to avoid problems with the leading zero, it is set up as a character field. However, there are many fields that need to be investigated if the inferred data type is different from the documented. Money or numeric fields may be inferred as character. Date fields may be inferred as VarChar. Remember, the great thing about profiling your data is the results are based on the data itself. Therefore, the inferred data type is the most accurate data type.

Null Rule Analysis

Null rule analysis is to look at columns containing nulls when their documented NULL rules state that nulls are not allowed. This happens when the data is initially loaded, and the null rule is turned off in order to avoid all the errors that would normally occur during the load process. It may also just be old or bad documentation. If you are about to move the data to another system and want to avoid the same issue, you may need to perform this analysis before you run into the problem.

Unique Analysis

These are columns whose values are more than 95 percent unique. These columns are potential primary keys or natural keys. Data modelers and DBAs are usually interested in unique analysis. Data modelers need to be relatively sure that the fields they think should be the key to the data can actually support the design. DBAs are interested for the same reason. The business user may be interested to see if the VIN or Social Security numbers are unique.

BUSINESS RULES

Some typical types of business rules include:

- **A set of rules for entering data in a database that is specific to an enterprise's methods of conducting its operations.** Business rules supplement rules for maintaining the domain and referential integrity of tables in a database.
- **Policies by which a business is run.** These business rules dictate the behavior of the business. These assertions define data from a business point of view. For example, the state code business rule might be the 50 United States, the District of Columbia, and the U.S. Territories. Another example is an insurance company that is only licensed to do business in ten states.
- **The descriptive statements of how a business is run.** These statements describe how the various entities relate to each other. One example would be the rule that states an accounts payable vendor could be one of three types: supplier, transportation provider, or governmental agency.
- **Narrative description of policies, procedures, or principles within an organization used to determine cardinality for entity relationship diagrams.** For example, a pilot cannot be on duty for more than ten hours during a 24-hour period.
- **Descriptions of the operations, definitions, and constraints that apply to an organization in achieving its goals.** For example, a business rule may state that no credit check is to be performed on return customers. Another may define a tenant in terms of solvency or list preferred suppliers and supply schedules.

As you can see, business rules pertain to how a business is run. Most business rules can be converted to data rules. For example, a valid set of values must exist for the state field or accounts payable vendor, or pilot duty must be less than or equal to ten.

While we've been touching on business rules throughout the book, let's now look at some specific types of business rules. These are rules that, while enforced by the application, many people are not even aware of because the application was developed years ago. There are also business rules that only the business analyst is aware of, usually because the IT organization does not dwell on the more detailed relationships in the business data. For example, an insurance company creates a separate but duplicate record when one of its customers passes away.

There are also many data rules, such as completeness rules. This can be confusing. When is a business rule a rule that can be applied to the data, and when is it just a data rule? Completeness is really checking to see if data exits in a field. It is not checking to see if the data itself is correct; only that the field is populated. The business rule is that the data should be populated if another field has a particular value. To me, it doesn't matter what you call them; rules are rules.

Completeness Rules

Completeness rules are one step beyond missing values analysis. How many of you had to fill out a medical form that asks a gender-specific question? Being male, I always laugh when I'm asked if I have ever been pregnant. In such a case, doing missing values analysis would not be as much value. However, if I did the analysis based upon gender, the results would be more meaningful. There are many completeness rules that can be designed to add a great deal of value to the business user.

Domain Constraints

Constraints are rules applied to the data. These rules are the tests to see if the constraints are being enforced. Domain constraints consist of a number of different types of rules. One rule might be a simple rule looking at the inferred data type. Is the

VIN number a character field? It's seems funny to be talking about a number as a character but so be it.

Another rule might be a range check. Are the salary figures for nonmanagement employees between ten thousand and forty thousand dollars? Are all the recruits born before a certain date; i.e., are they at least eighteen years of age? Is there a set of valid values that exist for the domain? There are only 62 valid state codes for an address. Is the data in that valid value set?

Dependency Constraints

Dependency constraints take domain constraints to another level. The number of valid values in the state column is dependent on the country code. If the country is United States, then the value should be one of 62 values. It the country is Canada, then there should be only 13 possible values – ten provinces and three territories. If I look at salary ranges, I may also want to look at salary grade. If I am look at loan length, I may also want to look at the type of loan (e.g., car, home, boat, etc.).

Derivation Rules

Calculated fields, as discussed earlier, are one kind of derivation rule. There are other types of derivation rules besides mathematical rules. For example, if I were to give you a list of symptoms, a doctor would derive my illness. Marketing departments use derivation rules to figure out how likely I am to purchase a product based upon past purchases of other similar products. My experience focuses on finding mathematical derivation rules in my customers' data.

Consistency Rules

Consistency rules are rules to determine if the wrong kinds of data are contained in the table or field; e.g., U.S. and international customers combined the same table. It is one thing to combine North American data in the same table, because the data generally shares the same rules. Telephone numbers all use the same North American Plan. Address data is similar. However, when you add European and Asian customer data, all the rules either become very complicated or break.

Consistency rules also apply when consumer and business customer data is kept in the same file.

Conformity Rules

Conformity rules determine how the data is stored. If the data is a money field, are all the data stored with the decimal point, or is it always implied? When you type in a phone number, which special characters, if any, are allowed in the field? Is all the data stored in upper case, lower case, or title case? Are the Social Security numbers stored with a dash between the subfields? What about your date fields? When profiling data of a large consumer bank, I found that one table had four different formats for date in the same record. This problem may have been both a conformity and a consistency issue with the data.

Chapter 5

PROFILING SPECIFIC TYPES OF DATA

LET'S now turn to profiling specific types of data. These might be money fields. On the surface, money is money, right? What about date fields? If it is valid data, it's fine, right? What do I do with free form text fields? This chapter walks you though the process to help you learn about these and other types of fields.

FREE FORM TEXT FIELDS

Free form text fields may be a comment field, product description, address fields, or other fields that contain more than one business fact. Some examples of free form text fields may be the name field that contains name prefix, first name, initial, surname, name suffix; or the product description field that contains brand, color, size, model, country or type, subtype, manufacturer, size, measurement, and part number. Unless there are a limited number of values, you have to parse the field to better analyze it.

A common problem with this type of data is that it is not described in the same way each time. For example, a product description may be described as manufacturer, size, type, subtype, and part number. Another time it may be described as part number, type, subtype, manufacturer, size, and measurement. Other times it may have values missing. Therefore, you need an intelligent parser to pick out the components into separate fields.

I am sure you have experienced issues with your own name, such as various iterations of your first name and initials. For example, I create various minor iterations of my name and address to help me identify the origin of junk mail. For example, I vary my room number (I work out of my house) in my address. Sometimes I am E. Lindsey. Other times I am Ed or Edward, using or eliminating my middle initial. I also vary the middle initial. Unless you parse this information out, you can never be sure if you have duplicate records.

Here is an example of what can happen if you do not parse the data and look for duplicate records in your data using fuzzy matching:

Another DVD Scam Revealed
Posted: November 14, 2003, 11:02 AM
Source: newsday.com.

It was too good a deal to pass up: buy one DVD at full price and get five more for 49 cents each. So good in fact that two brothers answered the newspaper ad, not just once, or twice, but 675 times, using a different name with each order, according to US police.

"I wouldn't be surprised if someone manages to steal five or 10 CDs," Det. Sgt. James Tilton, deputy commander of the Nassau's Crimes Against Property Squad, said of the relatively simple scam. "But something of this magnitude..."

Police estimate that brothers William Linsner, 29, of 72 Pond Rd. in Woodbury and George Linsner, 37, of 4327 223rd St., Bayside, bilked about 3,200 DVDs worth more than $60,000 from the music club which direct markets CDs, DVDs, and videos.

The brothers then sold them on the Internet for $5 to $10 each, police said.

"Their motives were just monetary, for personal benefit," Tilton said.

Since March, the brothers ordered the merchandise and had it sent to several addresses but mostly to their mother's home in

Elmont, police said. Columbia House officials in Indiana became suspicious in October after none of the bills for DVDs were paid, Tilton said. The company then contacted U.S. postal officials who investigated the incident in conjunction with police.

Reached by phone Thursday, a woman who identified herself as the brothers' mother said she had no comment.

"She's an elderly woman and knew nothing about it," Tilton said.

The brothers were arraigned Thursday and charged with second-degree larceny, punishable by up to 10 years in prison, and computer trespass, for which they could serve up to four years, if found guilty. Neither could be reached for comment.

Both were released with supervision and are due back in court Monday.

The whole purpose of parsing this information out is to find anomalies in your data. There are multiple ways of spelling a color, product description, or duplicate entries. If I were looking for duplicates in the data, almost 700 instances of the same address would cause me some concern. It is difficult to find anomalies if you do not standardize the way the data is represented.

CHANGES IN STATE

You need to be aware of how changes in state are accounted for in the data. Here are some typical changes in state for an employee.

- Hired -> Active -> Retired
- Hired -> Active -> Terminated
- Hired -> Active -> Quit
- Rehired -> Active -> Retired
- Rehired -> Active -> Quit

- Rehired -> Active -> Terminated

Does the company move the employee record out of the active system and into a retired or terminated file? On the other hand, does the employee record have a status indicator?

I was working at an insurance company and noticed they had a number of duplicate customer numbers in their data. Of course, the first time I saw this I immediately assumed this was an error. Most of the employees at the customer site thought the same thing. However, upon further investigation, it was explained to us that the system adds a customer record with a different status when a customer dies. Once the claim is paid out, the active records are moved to another system while the new deceased record is retained for a number of years.

When working with this company, I had another business rule to add. I checked the status and looked for a date in the termination field. If the status was deceased, I expected to find a valid date. If the status was active, I expected to find this field empty. If the status was cancelled, I expected to find a date in the termination field, but I also expected to find no additional record added to the file. Ninety days after the termination date, all of the cancelled records were moved to a cancelled policy system. After that, a new record had to be created, and new rates were in effect if the customer wanted to be covered again.

DATES

I contacted a company's tech support to complain that my software would not install. The company promised to send a replacement CD under the warranty, but nothing showed up. While checking into the matter, I had difficulties finding my record because I had reported the defect on one date but the trouble ticket was dated the next day in the company's system. The reason: my original call happened at 11:00 PM California time, but the company's system is somewhere in Texas where it was 1:00 AM the next day. What's the lesson here? Go to bed early or always display dates and other user-related data in terms that relate to the user's circumstances and not to your own system's internal records.

When profiling dates, it is always good to known how and when the date information is recorded. For example, an airfreight company owns a large fleet of planes. When the company loads data into its maintenance system, all the date fields are loaded with a date of 01/01/9999. This way, the company knows that a specific maintenance routine has not been performed yet.

Inferred Data Type

When profiling a date field, the first property of a date field I look at is the inferred data type. Does the software actually infer the field to be a date field, or a character field, or a numerical field? If the software does not infer it as a date, it usually means that the data does not contain valid dates. Invalid dates may be very old dates or dates somewhere in the future. These values (the minimum and maximum allowable date) should be configurable in the software. For example, one company has customers that are validated for life. This lifetime validation is indicated in the data with an expiration date of 12/31/9999. For the profiling software to accept this date, I needed to change the maximum date to 12/31/9999. Another option would be to write a business rule that would test the data type <> date or date field <> 12/31/9999. This way I would find the other out of range dates but allow the 12/31/9999 date.

Note: <> means not equal

Format

After I verify that the field is considered a date, I then look at the format of the date. Is it inferred as a U.S. date (i.e., month, day, and year) or a European date (i.e., day, month, and year) or some other format? Here are some possible formats:

- mdy2   Numeric date as mmddyy
- xmdy2   Numeric date as mddyy or mmddyy
- dmy2   Numeric date as ddmmyy
- xdmy2   Numeric date as dmmyy or ddmmyy
- ymd2   Numeric date as yymmdd
- mdy4   Numeric date as mmddyyyy
- xmdy4   Numeric date as mddyyyy or mmddyyyy
- dmy4   Numeric date as ddmmyyyy
- xdmy4   Numeric date as dmmyyyy or ddmmyyyy
- ymd4   Numeric date as yyyymmdd
- ym2   Numeric date as yymm
- ym4   Numeric date as yyyymm
- my2   Numeric date as mmyy
- my4   Numeric date as mmyyyy
- jul1   Numeric julian date as yddd
- jul2   Numeric julian date as yyddd
- jul4   Numeric julian date as yyyyddd
- week1   Numeric week date as ywwd
- week2   Numeric week date as yywwd
- week4   Numeric week date as yyyywwd
- cmdy2   Numeric date w/century indicator as cmmddyy
- cymd2   Numeric date w/century indicator as cyymmdd
- mdyc2   Numeric date w/century indicator as mmddyyc
- dmyc2   Numeric date w/century indicator as ddmmyyc
- ymdc2   Numeric date w/century indicator as yymmddc

This list is not complete but shows some of the different possible variations. Also, remember to consider the special characters that separate the components of the date, e.g., slash, period, dash, etc.

Patterns

Pattern analysis shows the answers to some of these questions and shows the frequencies of the different formats. Here is an example in Table 5.1:

Patterns	Matching	Frequency
99/99/9999	171	1.69%
9/9/9999	103	1.02%
99/9/9999	20	0.19%
9/99/9999	13	0.12%

Table 5.1

This shows that the data is in the same format, but you may want to standardize the dates to two-digit months and days.

Min/Max

Minimum and maximum values in dates also show potential outliers. If you are looking at customer birth dates, do you have minimum dates that identify customers that are over 100 years old? Is the birth date greater than today by looking at maximum values? When you look at hire dates, are they before the company was founded?

Cross-Field Analysis

Do you have multiple date fields that have a relationship? For example, do you have a trade date and a settlement date in your record? You can compare the dates and make sure that your trade date is before your settlement date. Is the hire date greater than the birth date? Is the hire date greater than the termination date?

Is the SPUD date greater than the Rig Release date? While working at a large overnight shipping company, I compared the ship date to the delivery date. You guessed it – the company delivered a portion of its packages before they were shipped. And no, these were not international shipments.

Cross-field analysis helps you identify errors and bad records. However, it still does not validate all other dates. For example, is the difference between trade date and settlement date equal to or greater than zero, but less than or equal to three? Cross-field analysis will help you find out.

Frequency Distributions

You can look at the frequency distributions of the dates to find dates automatically generated by the system or a default date. Frequency distributions can be used to find dates that the operator generated quickly like 01/01/01. Is there an even distribution of dates or dates of busy days? If you look at days of the week, does Tuesday afternoon have a lower distribution of values than days like Saturday or Friday night? In financial data, sometimes you notice a spike at month end or quarter end where all of the adjustments are bunched up around book closing. Are the paycheck dates weekly, biweekly, or monthly? Are there dates that do not fall into this normal distribution of dates?

Bank Holidays/Sundays

When looking at dates, do any business transactions fall on a Sunday (assuming the business is closed on Sundays)? Earlier in the book, we looked at dates that included Saturday and Sundays for financial transactions. Are there national holidays or bank holidays when you do not expect to do business, but you see transactions on the date? I was profiling a large electronics retailer's data and found store closings that happened at four o'clock in the morning. These were highlighted and discussed with the business user. It turns out that these were valid times. Some stores closed at midnight and continued restocking for the next couple of hours. The store remained in operation but was just not open to the public. The store was finally closed by the manager at four in the morning.

Durations

Duration of dates refer to a duration of time when an event was happening. One example is a marketing campaign. You offer a special for the month of June when this type of sale is valid. Grocery store chains have weekly sales circulars. Now you need to know if the sales run from Wednesday to Tuesday, or Sunday to Saturday.

For example, let's say I am offering a discount that is valid only if purchased in June. If I am looking at the records that have a discount value of JUN-PROMO, are the dates only in June? If I am offering a birthday special, did it occur on the birthday of the individual customer or within the month of the customer's birthday?

Clusters

Clusters of dates can also help you find anomalies in your data. Usually, the best ways to view clusters are via a chart or a range check. Are all my employees between the ages of eighteen and fifty-five? Are all airline pilots between twenty-one and sixty? Are there specific clusters that do not look correct? Clusters also point out busy times, which is nice to know but not something you usually use data profiling to find out.

Figure 5.1 shows an example of salary data. You notice right off that the values do not look right. There are many values in the 5.25 to 13 range, and many values in the 25,000 to 150,000 range. After further scrutiny and discussing this finding with the business user, it was determined that both annual salary and hourly pay were included in the same field. There is another column in the table that determines the pay rate. This is permissible in the current application because it is able to handle mixed data, but moving it to another application may cause problems. You may have determined this by looking at the minimum and maximum values, but the frequencies were pretty disbursed. The chart clearly highlights the differences.

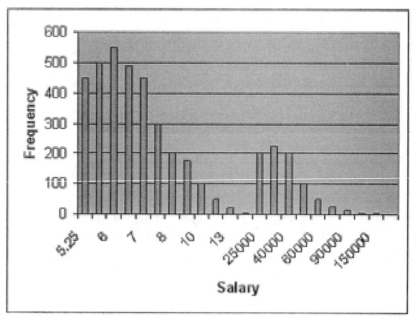

Figure 5.1

Time

Time values are like dates, and most of the analysis techniques discussed thus far apply. However, one special characteristic of time needs to be mentioned. You need to be aware of time zones and military time. When you look at time stamps, do they include time zone? When you calculate differences in time, are you comparing the same time zone? The same is true of military time. Are you comparing 0900 to 9:00 PM? As discussed earlier, are you looking at the local time of the event occurrence, or are you looking at the time generated by the system clock of the centralized system?

Money

A database server stores money values as decimal values. The precision parameter defines the total number of significant digits, and the scale parameter defines the total number of digits to the right of the decimal separator. For example, if you define a column as money (8,3), the column can contain a maximum of eight digits, and three of these digits are to the right of the decimal separator. An example of a data value in the column might be 12345.678.

The real problem with money fields is that they all look alike on the surface: dealer cost, invoice amount, paycheck fields, insurance premiums, item cost, phone bill amount, etc. This section shows you how to use different techniques to spot anomalies to help you improve the quality of your money-related data.

Data Type

To spot anomalies in data, the first thing I look at is the data type. Does the software infer a numeric or decimal data type? If it is a numeric data type, is the decimal implied? By this I mean is the period not stored, but when you do anything with the data, are there cents involved? Is the data type decimal, numeric, or money? What is the precision? Does the business deal with tenths or hundreds of a penny? If the data type is Char or VarChar, are there special characters imbedded in the data, or is there bad data in the column?

Patterns

Next, I look at the patterns of the data. Do the patterns look something like these in Table 5.2?

Patterns	Matching	Frequency
99.99	3794645	35.91%
999.99	3763787	35.62%
9	2373390	22.46%
9999.99	390011	3.69%
-999.99	237555	2.24%
9.99	4031	0.03%
-9999.99	2122	0.02%
-9.99	865	0.01%
-99.99	43	0.01%

Table 5.2

Here I can see that the decimal point is embedded in the data. I also see that some of the values are negative numbers. Are the values in the expected range?

Negative Numbers

As shown in Table 5.2, negative numbers are easily identifiable in pattern analysis and as shown in the value frequencies. I always sort on the values to show me the top and bottom ten values. I also look at the minimum and maximum values. Are negative numbers allowable? Is this the way that product returns and refunds are accounted for? Are vendors paid out of the register? I always do a sort on the values and look for the highs and lows. The lows will spot the negative numbers immediately.

Ranges

When dealing with money fields, ranges are a quick way to find problems. If I am selling appliances, are all my transactions in the range of two hundred dollars to two thousand dollars? Maybe I would like to check the ranges of commissions for individual sales reps. What about the range of transactions by manufacturer? Am I paying one vendor significantly more on a monthly basis than others? On the other hand, am I paying someone a lot less for the same quantities of merchandise (such as in the case of money laundering)? I had a friend who owned a restaurant with questionable associates. He paid for all his provisions in cash and never showed the invoices on the books. On paper, his business was a huge financial success. While I may have found issues with his business practices, I may not have found issues with his data. You need to understand the nature of the business for these ranges to make sense.

Frequency Distributions

Value	Frequency	Percent
0	2373390	22.46%
40.00	513661	4.86%
231.00	428992	4.05%
19.30	362788	3.43%

37.50	315065	2.98%
13.86	291104	2.75%
14.25	243154	2.30%
14.90	201060	1.90%
35.00	185982	1.76%
176.00	180466	1.70%
Value	**Frequency**	**Percent**
-1600.00	1	0.01%
-976.00	1	0.01%
-941.00	1	0.01%
-539.00	1	0.01%
-427.00	1	0.01%
-365.00	1	0.01%
-337.00	1	0.01%
-332.00	1	0.01%
-211.00	1	0.01%
-163.00	1	0.01%
-142.00	1	0.01%

Table 5.3

Table 5.3 shows a list of the most and least frequent values. As you can see, the most frequent value is zero. Normally this might not be an issue; however, this field represents the dealer cost. The least frequent values are very large negative numbers. Least frequent values are always suspect. The least frequent value may be a typo. The most frequent values may be the default values.

Top and Bottom 10 Values

Using this same data, here are the top and bottom ten values:

Value	Frequency	Percent
-2000.00	696	0.01%
-1994.00	18	0.01%
-1990.00	191	0.01%
-1600.00	1	0.01%
-1490.00	6	0.01%
-1300.00	7	0.01%
-1294.00	17	0.01%
-1290.00	77	0.01%
-1240.00	2	0.01%
-1200.00	103	0.01%
Value	Frequency	Percent
5274.00	123	0.01%
5330.00	82	0.01%
5378.00	59	0.01%
5620.00	255	0.01%

5784.00	236	0.01%
5803.00	104	0.01%
5815.00	15	0.01%
6192.00	88	0.01%
6726.00	247	0.01%
6996.00	304	0.01%

Table 5.4

When I look at the top and bottom values in a money field displayed in Table 5.4, I start to wonder, "Can I have dealer cost on a product that has negative numbers? Do I have products that cost almost seven thousand dollars?" Here the numbers show one thing, but because the frequency of those values is relatively high, I may not be inclined to believe that there is a typo. When looking at the top and bottom ten of the frequency, I might think differently.

Cross Field Analysis

With money fields, cross-field analysis can be a good way to find anomalies. Are there certain types of products that should have a low dealer cost? I might do a range check by type of product. The same is true of management level and salary. I could check employee department and see if anyone other than the sales department has a commission amount in the paycheck field. If hourly and annual compensation is stored in the same file but in different fields, you can make sure both fields are not populated for the same employee, and the proper field is populated based upon the pay type.

(Pay_Type = 'A' and YR_Comp IS NULL)
OR
(Pay_Type = 'H' and HR_Pay IS NULL)
OR
(HR_Pay IS NULL and YR_Comp IS NULL)
OR
(HR_Pay IS NOT NULL and YR_Comp IS NOT NULL)

Another example of cross-field analysis is between a field or fields to determine if a money field should be zero or have a value. The life insurance payout amount field should not be populated if the customer is still alive. What about invoice amount for inactive or ineligible customers? These do not show up in table analysis because the other types of values have different money values and, as such, do not show a relationship.

Cross Field Relationships

Cross-field relationships are different in that these are specific relationships that exist (or should exist) between fields in the record. Calculated fields are the primary example. For example, is there a total cost field that is calculated using item cost and quantity? Is there a bank deposit field that is calculated using individual check amounts? What about a paycheck field that is calculated using salary minus taxes and benefits? These may show up during table analysis, but probably won't for the last example because each employee has different benefits and occupy different tax brackets.

Clusters

Are all my salaries with in certain clusters? As shown in Table 5.1 earlier in this chapter, hourly and exempt salaries can be stored in the same file. Clusters point out a large spike in single digit wages for the hourly employees versus the employees who fall into the forty thousand to ninety thousand dollar exempt bracket.

While this is not necessarily an anomaly, it does indicate mixed data in the file. You need to be aware of this when you move the data to a new system. You may want to separate the information to avoid confusion and potential bad business decisions. Obviously, the data works fine in the application because the cross-field relationships are enforced by the application. However, when you repurpose the data, you open yourself up to a completely new set of problems.

STANDARDIZATION

I identify standardization issues in nearly every data profiling project. These issues can be simple, such as mixed case, to more complex problems, such as when multiple names represent the same business fact (e.g., customer name, corporate name, product description, etc.) The classic example is:

    AT&T
    att
    ATT
    American Telephone and Telegraph

Or street

    Street
    street
    St.
    St
    ST
    street

I never ask for the data to be modified before the initial profiling. This is for two reasons. One, I want to see the potential standardization issues as the data is stored and want to document them. Two, I am always afraid that the process will introduce anomalies during the "correction" process. That said, I do like to see some standardization done to the data after the initial profiling process is complete.

Normally, the company will not go back to the source and make the corrections there. The possibility of breaking something in the application is too great. Normally, the company will do another extraction of the data, making the corrections and standardization in the process.

I like this process for a few of reasons. First, I am able to test the standardization/correction process. If some of the relationships that existed before the standardization process are now broken, then something went wrong. In addition, I can check the valid values and see if all of them have been repaired. Finally, I can find additional relationships that did not exist before.

A typical standardization example is two state fields that now have the same information. One may be a three-digit numeric Federal Information Processing Standards (FIPS) code, or a two-character United States Postal Service (USPS) code, or the full name may be spelled out. When the data is standardized, it should show a significant overlap in values. Also, it is easier to check against reference data if all of the fields contain the same form of representation.

There are other types of standardization I like to see after the initial profiling has been completed, such as converting everything to the same case, upper or lower. One energy customer I was working with stored the county name in three ways: spelled out, abbreviated, and as the three-digit county code. After standardization, the data had a much higher cross-table redundancy with other data fields. Standardization is also very important when looking for duplicate records.

Business and Consumer Data Mixed

Many times when profiling data, I find that there is only one customer file. Both business and individual consumer customers are lumped together. The reason is unimportant. I find there are different relationships for one type of customer versus the other type of customer.

For example, when I am purchasing something online, I am sometimes required to enter a company name, even thought I am purchasing it for myself. As a consumer customer, I should be able to leave the company name field blank.

Now that you have read thus far in this book, you can imagine what I do in this scenario. I enter one of the companies I worked for previously, or RoboForm automatically enters the data. Alternatively, I may suddenly decide to be the president of GE or the director of the CIA.

I am sure you can think of other relationships that might be different between your consumer and corporate data – for example, credit limit, driver license information, birth date, etc.

After profiling all the data, I go back and reprofile it using a where clause if there is a field that is used to identify the type of customer. This gives me a different insight into the data. I discussed this earlier in the section on segmentation. I also develop different business rules or much more complicated rules to cover all possibilities in the data. For example, do my consumer customers have a null value in company name? Are the minimum and maximum values for consumer different for the entire population of the data?

MISFILED DATA

Misfiled data is another example of specialized standardization. Let's look at an example in the fields address1, address2, and address3. The first problem is that this data design process needs to be more specific. Normally I expect to find the street address in address1, additional street address in address2, and city, state, and ZIP code in address3.

In reality, I find all kinds of address data in all of the fields. Most data quality software takes this problem into account and allows you to enter three to five fields into the algorithm for address validation. But it also makes profiling the data difficult.

After profiling the data, I recommend you try to standardize the data stored in particular fields. I also recommend you parse out as much information as possible into more intelligently designed fields. Simple parsing includes moving city, state, and ZIP information to their own fields. You may also want to separate street address and PO box information into separate fields. If a company uses a PO box to receive mail, I find that the United States Postal Service returns mail with a street address, even if that street address exists.

Parsing is also important for product descriptions with such free form text fields as brand, color, size, model, country, or type, subtype, manufacturer, size, measurement, and part number. These fields should be broken out to the best of your abilities. I recommend parsing not only for profiling. Since you are probably repurposing the data, you may want to query your data based upon some of this information. I know I would want to know how ruby red lipstick is selling in Toledo, Ohio.

UNIT OF MEASURE

Remember the NASA story about the confusion between feet and meters? The unit of measure in which information is stored may not be an important issue during profiling, but is a very important issue in the long run. Data in the system needs to be stored in the same unit of measure. When doing cross-table analysis, you may get invalid results if the data is stored differently in the two systems with which you are working.

The NASA example points out a serious problem with storing feet and meters in the same system. Another example is storing money in different currencies. I would love to use my ATM card in Europe to withdraw euros while my U.S. bank withdraws dollars from my account without having to perform a currency conversion.

I remember hearing a story of a mechanic working on a tank during the first Gulf War. He needed a part in order to complete repairs, so he used a provisioning system that was available to him in Iraq. He ordered one box of the part in question. After two days, his sergeant chewed him out for not having the tank repaired and back in action. He went back to the provisioning system and expedited the order. Two days latter an airfreight truck pulled up and asked where he wanted the delivery.

He said he would take it right there, as he needed to repair the tank ASAP. The driver laughed. He said, "You idiot, the entire tractor-trailer truckload is yours. You ordered a boxcar load of the parts." This is just another example of the importance of standardizing on size. Is the data represented as single unit, packet, box, pallet, trailer, or tanker, etc? When you start using RFID data, is the ID for a box, case, or pallet?

Chapter 6

SPECIAL DATA VALUE ANALYSIS

Vehicle Identification Number (VIN)

A **VIN** is currently made up of 17 characters or digits, each with a particular purpose. Table 6.1 shows the structure of the data comprising a VIN.

VIN Structure		
Position	ISO	North America
1-3	WMI	Manufacturer Identifier
4-8	VDS	Vehicle Attributes
9	VDS	Check Digit
10	VIS	Model Year
11	VIS	Plant Code
12-17	VIS	Sequential Number

Table 6.1

Let's review the breakdown of the data comprising a VIN in more detail.

The first three positions vary slightly depending on whether you are using the North American standard or the ISO 3779 format. In the North American standard, the first position identifies where the vehicle was manufactured, while the ISO standard uses the first two positions.

WMI Region Notes

A-H Africa AA-AH = South Africa
J-R Asia J = Japan
KL-KR = South Korea
L = China
MA-ME = India
MF-MK = Indonesia
ML-MR = Thailand
PA-PE = Philippines
PL-PR = Malaysia
S-Z Europe SA-SM = United Kingdom
SN-ST, W = Germany
SU-SZ = Poland
TA-TH = Switzerland
TJ-TP = Czech Republic
TR-TV = Hungary
VA-VE = Austria
VF-VR = France
VS-VW = Spain
VX-V2 = Yugoslavia
XS-XW = USSR
X3-X0 = Russia
YA-YE = Belgium
YF-YK = Finland
YS-YW = Sweden
ZA-ZR = Italy
1-5 North America 1, 4, 5 = United States
2 = Canada
3 = Mexico
6-7 Oceania 6A-6W = Australia

7A-7E = New Zealand
8-0 South America 8A-8E = Argentina
8F-8J = Chile
8X-82 = Venezuela
9A-9E, 93-99 = Brazil
9F-9J = Colombia

The second position identifies the vehicle's manufacturer, for example:
Audi (A)
BMW (B)
Buick (4)
Cadillac (6)
Chevrolet (1)
Chrysler (C)
Dodge (B)
Ford (F)
GM Canada (7)
General Motors (G)
Honda (H)
Jaguar (A)
Lincoln (L)
Mercedes Benz (D)
Mercury (M)
Nissan (N)
Oldsmobile (3)
Pontiac (2 or 5)
Plymouth (P)
Saturn (8)
Toyota (T)
Volkswagen (V)
Volvo(V)

The third position identifies the vehicle type or manufacturing division.

The fourth through eighth positions identify vehicle features, such as body style, engine type, model, series, etc.

One manufacturer's data breaks down as follows:

- Fourth position = model by body type (sedan, coupe, lift back, wagon, and convertible)
- Fifth position = engine size
- Sixth position = grade
- Seventh position = the type of restraint system installed (e.g., number of airbags)
- Eighth position = the line or model
- Ninth position = VIN accuracy as check digit
- Tenth position = the model year
- Eleventh position = the assembly plant for the vehicle
- Twelfth through seventeenth positions = the sequence of the vehicle for production as it rolled of the manufacturer's assembly line

Table 6.2 shows the codes for the model year. Note that the VIN number breaks in 2010 and a change will be required.

Model Year

Code	Year	Code	Year	Code	Year
A	1980	L	1990	Y	2000
B	1981	M	1991	1	2001
C	1982	N	1992	2	2002
D	1983	P	1993	3	2003
E	1984	R	1994	4	2004
F	1985	S	1995	5	2005
G	1986	T	1996	6	2006
H	1987	V	1997	7	2007
J	1988	W	1998	8	2008
K	1989	X	1999	9	2009

Table 6.2

Let's break down the VIN number for a Toyota.

```
1 2 3 4 5 6 7 8 9 0 1 2 3 4 5 6 7
2 T 1 K R 3 2 E 0 5 C 3 0 A 6 5 0
```

This vehicle was manufactured in Canada.
By Toyota in the Plant in Cambridge Ontario, Canada
With a 1.8L engine
Model Year - 2005
Model Corolla
Two airbags

Profiling

When I begin profiling the VIN number, I start with data type. Is it a Char (17)? If the inferred data type is anything else, I know there is a problem. If it is VarChar, then I know every value less than or greater than seventeen is a problem.

Then I look at uniqueness. If I am dealing with a vehicle inventory, then I better have only one VIN for each vehicle in stock. If I am dealing with a fleet of vehicles and I am tracking maintenance, then duplicates are okay for maintenance records. However, a high frequency on a couple of VIN numbers might indicate a lemon, or someone might keep putting in the same VIN for routine work and does not want to capture the actual VIN.

Keeping with the maintenance record example, I use the engine size indicator in the VIN to compare it to a tune-up record. Am I being charged for an 8-cylinder tune-up when the engine is only a 4-cylinder? In addition, I use the VIN to validate the model year field.

I parse the VIN characters looking for the letters I, O, and Q that are invalid in a VIN number.

I then build a list of valid manufacturers and manufacturer-dependent vehicle attributes and test the VIN. For example, I let's say I'm testing for invalid Toyota manufacturer identifiers where:

```
SUBSTR(VEH_SER_NBR,1,3) <> '1NX' AND
SUBSTR(VEH_SER_NBR,1,3) <> 'JTD' AND
SUBSTR(VEH_SER_NBR,1,3) <> 'JTE' AND
SUBSTR(VEH_SER_NBR,1,3) <> 'JTK' AND
SUBSTR(VEH_SER_NBR,1,3) <> 'JTL' AND
SUBSTR(VEH_SER_NBR,1,3) <> 'JT2' AND
SUBSTR(VEH_SER_NBR,1,3) <> 'JT3' AND
SUBSTR(VEH_SER_NBR,1,3) <> '2T1' AND
SUBSTR(VEH_SER_NBR,1,3) <> '4T1' AND
SUBSTR(VEH_SER_NBR,1,3) <> '4T3' AND
SUBSTR(VEH_SER_NBR,1,3) <> '5TB' AND
SUBSTR(VEH_SER_NBR,1,3) <> '5TD' AND
SUBSTR(VEH_SER_NBR,1,3) <> '5TE' AND
SUBSTR(VEH_SER_NBR,1,3) <> 'JTM' AND
SUBSTR(VEH_SER_NBR,1,3) <> 'JTN' AND
SUBSTR(VEH_SER_NBR,1,3) <> '3TM' AND
SUBSTR(VEH_SER_NBR,1,3) <> '5TF'
```

I could calculate a check digit for the VIN and compare it to the check digit contained in the VIN.

You could look for U, Z or 0 in model year, which are currently invalid.

Pattern analysis helps very little. You get values that look like the ones in Table 6.3.

Patterns	Matching	Frequency
9U9UU99U99U9(6)	450426	30.40%
9UUUU99U99U9(6)	381753	25.77%
U(5)99U9(9)	300867	20.31%
9UUUU9(5)U9(6)	90800	6.12%
U(5)9(12)	85955	5.80%
9U9UU99UU9U9(6)	45091	3.04%
9UUUU99UU9U9(6)	37923	2.56%
U(5)99UU9(8)	30048	2.02%
9U9UU99U99U99U999	17609	1.18%
9UUUU99U99U99U999	11230	0.75%
9UUUU999U9U9(6)	9308	0.62%
U(5)999U9(8)	8687	0.58%
9UUUU9(5)U99U999	4982	0.33%
UU9UU99U9(9)	2942	0.19%
9U9UU99UU9U99U999	1722	0.11%
9UUUU99UU9U99U999	1126	0.07%

9UUUU999U9U99U999	488	0.03%
UU9UU99UU9(8)	313	0.02%
9U9UU99U9UU9(6)	13	0.01%
9UUUU99U9UU9(6)	13	0.01%
9U9UU99U9UU99U999	4	0.01%
UU9UU99U9U9(7)	3	0.01%

Table 6.3

A VIN has a wealth of information that can be used to cross-check both the VIN itself and other columns within your data. How you use this information depends on the detail you wish to pursue in trying to ferret out issues with the data.

LICENSE PLATES

License plate data can be extremely important, and accuracy is critical. For example, let's say you're a police department. To identify stolen vehicles, you must have accurate license plates.

Let's look at some examples of standard-issue passenger plate numbering. Note that a hyphen indicates either a dash or other divider or a space between numbers.

1234	Used in American Samoa currently
12345	Used in Rhode Island currently
12345N	Used currently in Nunavut, a territory in Canada; letter is always "N"
123456	Used in Delaware and the Northwest Territories currently
123-456	Used in New Hampshire in the early 2000s)
123-4567	Used in New Hampshire currently and in Illinois in the early 2000s
1234-AB	Used in Maine currently and in Massachusetts in the early 2000s
1234-ABC	Used in Georgia in the early 2000s and New York in the late 1970s
123-ABC	Used in Arkansas, Arizona, British Columbia, Colorado, Connecticut, Kentucky, Mississippi, Nevada, New Mexico, Oklahoma, Oregon, Saskatchewan, South Carolina, Tennessee, Texas, Utah, Washington, Wisconsin, and Quebec currently
12-A345	County-coded; used in Nebraska currently
12-A3456	County-coded; used in Montana currently
12A-345	County-coded; used in South Dakota currently
12A-B34	Date coded; last digit denotes month of expiration; used in Massachusetts currently
12A235B	County-coded; used in Alabama currently
12A3B4C	County-coded; used in Alabama currently as overflow for one county
12A1234	County-coded; used in Indiana currently
1-A2345	County-coded; used in Nebraska currently
1-A23456	County-coded; used in Montana currently
1A-23456	County-coded; used in Idaho currently
1A2345B	County-coded; used in Alabama currently
1AB-234	County-coded; used in South Dakota currently

1AB-234,
OAB-234,
NAB-234,
DAB-234   Date-coded; first digit or letter O for October, N for November, or D for December indicates month of expiration; used in West Virginia currently

1A-B2345   County-coded; used in Idaho currently

1AB-23C   Used in Missouri currently

1AB-C23   Used in Maryland currently and on Michigan "Great Lakes Splendor" plates currently

1A-BC234   County-coded; used in Idaho currently

1AB123   County-coded; used in Indiana currently as overflow for one county

1ABC234   Used in California currently

A-123456   County-coded; used in Idaho currently

A12-3456   Used in Illinois currently

A12-3BC   Used in Florida currently

A12-BCD   Used in Florida and Texas in the late 1990s and early 2000s

AB-12   (used in Rhode Island currently

AB-123   (used in Prince Edward Island and Rhode Island currently

AB-1234   Used in Washington, D.C. currently, in Connecticut from the 1960s through the 1980s

AB-123C   Used in New Jersey in the 1990s

AB12CD   Used in Ohio in the early 2000s

ABC12   Used in Yukon currently

ABC123   Used in New Mexico currently

ABC-123   Used in Alaska, Alberta, Manitoba, Hawaii, Kansas, Louisiana, Minnesota, Nebraska, New Brunswick, Newfoundland, North Dakota, Nova Scotia, Oklahoma, and Vermont currently

ABC1234   Used in Michigan c. 2004-2006

ABC-1234   Used in Georgia, Michigan, New York, North Carolina, Ohio, Pennsylvania, and Virginia currently

ABC-12D   Used in New Jersey in the 1980s (blue plates and
           currently (yellow plates , as well as in Florida and
           Texas in the early 1990s
ABCD-123   Used in Ontario currently

Armed with this information, you can segment the data (or use detailed cross-field analysis) and use pattern analysis to help identify anomalies in the field. Unfortunately, using most other metadata provides little assistance in trying to assess the data quality. For example, lengths are different and not all states are alphanumeric.

For additional information, contact you local department of motor vehicles or you can purchase

The Official License Plate Book 2002: A Complete Plate Identification Resource (License Plate Book) (Paperback) by Thomson C. Murray.

Driver's Licenses

Several states, including Florida, Wisconsin, Illinois, encode driver's license numbers with such data name, gender, and date of birth. If you look at a driver's license number issued by one of these states, you can make a good guess at the person's name and determine gender and date of birth. Conversely, if you have a name, date of birth, and gender, you can validate some or all of a person's driver's license number.

When you remove the hyphens, these license numbers look like this:

SSSSFFFYYDDD
F25592150094

The state-specific licenses look like this:

Florida:

SSSS-FFF-YY-DDD-N
F255-921-50-094-0

Illinois Driver's License:

SSSS-FFFY-YDDD
F255-9215-0094

Illinois State ID:

SSSF-FFYY-DDDS
2559-2150-094F

Wisconsin:

SSSS-FFFY-YDDD-NN
F255-9215-0121-03

In the Florida example, each data segment breaks down like this:

SSSS F255	Soundex code
FFF 921	First name, middle initial
YY 50	Year of birth
DDD 094	Day and month of birth
NN 03	Overflow (not all states use this)
SSSS	Soundex code of last name

Soundex is a hashing system for English words. Here is a quick look at how it works.

- Capitalize all letters in the word and drop all punctuation marks. Pad the word with rightmost blanks as needed during each procedure step.
- Retain the first letter of the word.
- Change all occurrence of the following letters to '0' (zero):

'A', 'E', 'I', 'O', 'U', 'H', 'W', 'Y'.

- Change letters from the following sets into the digit given:

1 = 'B', 'F', 'P', 'V'
2 = 'C', 'G', 'J', 'K', 'Q', 'S', 'X', 'Z'
3 = 'D','T'
4 = 'L'
5 = 'M','N'
6 = 'R'

- Remove all pairs of digits that occur beside each other from the string that resulted after step (4).
- Remove all zeros from the string that results from step 5.0 (placed there in step 3)
- Pad the string that resulted from step (6) with trailing zeros and return only the first four positions, which will be of the form <uppercase letter> <digit> <digit> <digit>.

Let's look at the data encoded in driver's license numbers and try to determine your license number.

FFF = first name and middle initial
Look up your first name in Table 6.4.

Name	Code	Name	Code	Name	Code
Albert	20	Frank	260	Marvin	580
Alice	20	George	300	Mary	580

Ann	40	Grace	300	Melvin	600
Anna	40	Harold	340	Mildred	600
Anne	40	Harriet	340	Patricia	680
Annie	40	Harry	360	Paul	680
Arthur	40	Hazel	360	Richard	740
Bernard	80	Helen	380	Robert	760
Bette	80	Henry	380	Ruby	740
Bettie	80	James	440	Ruth	760
Betty	80	Jane	440	Thelma	820
Carl	120	Jayne	440	Thomas	820
Catherine	120	Jean	460	Walter	900
Charles	140	Joan	480	Wanda	900
Dorothy	180	John	460	William	920
Edward	220	Joseph	480	Wilma	920
Elizabeth	220	Margaret	560		
Florence	260	Martin	560		
Donald	180				
Clara	140				

Table 6.4

If you can't find your name above, look up your first initial in Table 6.5.

Initial	Code	Initial	Code	Initial	Code	Initial	Code
A	0	H	320	O	640	V	860
B	60	I	400	P	660	W	880
C	100	J	420	Q	700	X	940
D	160	K	500	R	720	Y	960
E	200	L	520	S	780	Z	980
F	240	M	540	T	800		
G	280	N	620	U	840		

Table 6.5

Now look up your middle initial in Table 6.6.

Initial	Code	Initial	Code	Initial	Code	Initial	Code
A	1	H	8	O	14	V	18
B	2	I	9	P	15	W	19
C	3	J	10	Q	15	X	19
D	4	K	11	R	16	Y	19
E	5	L	12	S	17	Z	19
F	6	M	13	T	18		
G	7	N	14	U	18		

Table 6.6

Now, add together the code for either your first name (if possible) or your first initial to the code for your middle initial.

Y-Y = Birth year

The two numbers together represent the year of your birth. If you are born in 1968, it should read "68." In Wisconsin drivers licenses, this is the easiest information to pick out and is often used to spot fakes.

DDD = Month and day of birth and gender
This portion encodes the month and day of your birth.

The general equation is:

153

General: (birth_month - 1) * month_multiplier + birth_day + gender_mod

Florida: (birth_month - 1) * 40 + birth_day + (male:0, female: 500)

Illinois: (birth_month - 1) * 31 + birth_day + (male:0, female: 600)

Wisconsin: (birth_month - 1) * 40 + birth_day + (male:0, female: 500)

Birth_month is the number of months into the year. January is 1, December is 12.

Month_multiplier varies by state. Illinois uses 31. Wisconsin and Florida both use 40.

Gender_mod varies by state. In Illinois men use 0, women use 600. In Wisconsin and Florida men use 0, women use 500.

If the result is less than 100, add zeroes to the left side to make it 3 digits. For example, January 1 is encoded as "001" for men in Illinois.

Overflow

In examining how data is encoded in driver's license numbers, you may notice that it is possible for two people with similar names to get identical driver's license numbers. For example, if "Joshua William Smith" and "Jack Wayne Snoddy" are born on the same day, they get the same Illinois driver's license number. Overflow numbers solve this problem. Overflow numbers are a simple sequential numbers that are appended to duplicate numbers.

Wisconsin prints the overflow number on your license. As a result, the last two digits of your Wisconsin license number represent the number of people who had the same license number as you (ignoring the last two digits), when you got your license.

Illinois does not print this information on driver's licenses. If Joshua William Smith is wanted by police and his driver's license number is flagged as such, Jack Wayne Snoddy may be briefly detained while the police check their records to sort out the shared number. I have been told that Illinois state databases include a two- or three-digit number to distinguish between different people with the same license.

The format for New Jersey driver's license numbers is:
Alll fffmm MMyye A is alpha, the rest are numeric

A = first letter of last name
lll = encoding of last name, starting with second letter,
fff = encoding of first name
mm = encoding of middle initial
MM = month of birth and sex

01 for January male
12 for December male
51 for January female
62 for December female

yy = year of birth (last 2 digits)
e = eye color, encoded as shown in Table 6.7

Value	Color
1	Black
2	Brown
3	Grey
4	Blue
5	Hazel
6	Green

Table 6.7

As you can see, there is a wealth of information in driver's license numbers that can be used to determine the license number itself as well as additional information, such as eye color, date of birth, and gender. But it's up to you to validate this information. You may want to contact the state(s) with which you do business to get the most up-to-date and accurate information regarding license numbers. For example, you can get a feed of valid driver license numbers from individual state(s). Also, there is a whole book published on state-by-state driver license information that you use as a trusted source to validate your data.

Driver's license number data needs to be validated before it can be segmented for data matching purposes in a data quality plan. Because of the variety of ways different states determine license numbers, profiling techniques do not help in validating the number itself unless you segment the data by state. Profiling is only good at assisting in validating other information in the record.

If you do segment your data, a state-by-state list on valid formats for driver's licenses is included in the appendix. A more detailed book on driver's license laws is also available.

INTERNATIONAL STANDARD BOOK NUMBER (ISBN)

Structure of ISBN

An ISBN used to consist of ten digits preceded by the letters ISBN. As of January 1, 2007 they consist of thirteen digits. This book has the following ISBN numbers assigned to it.

International Standard Book Number 13 digit:
978-0-9800833-0-9

International Standard Book Number 10 digit:
0-9800833-0-3

Note: In countries where the Latin alphabet is not used, an abbreviation in the characters of the local script may be used in addition to the Latin letters ISBN.

The 10-digit number is divided into four parts of variable length, which must be separated clearly by hyphens or spaces. ISBN 10s cannot be converted only by adding the "978" prefix to the ISBN 10. The ISBN 13 do not only have the "978" prefix preceding the ISBN, but the check digit of the ISBN 10 is dropped and a new algorithm is applied to calculate a new check digit.

ISBN 0 571 08989 5 or ISBN 90-70002-04-3

Note: Experience suggests that hyphens are preferable
to spaces.

The number of digits in the first three parts of the ISBN (i.e., group identifier, publisher identifier, and title identifier) varies. The number of digits in the group number and in the publisher identifier is determined by the quantity of titles planned to be produced by the publisher or publisher group. Publishers or publisher groups with large title outputs are represented by fewer digits.

Group Identifier

The first part of the ISBN identifies a country, area, or language area participating in the ISBN system. Some members form language areas (e.g., group number 3 = German language group) or regional units (e.g., South Pacific = group number 982). A group identifier may consist of up to five digits.

Example:

ISBN 90- ... All group identifiers are allocated by the International ISBN Agency in Berlin.

Publisher Identifier

The second part of the ISBN identifies a particular publisher within a group. The publisher identifier usually indicates the exact identification of the publishing house and its address. If publishers exhaust their initial contingent of title numbers, they may be allocated an additional publisher identifier. The publisher identifier may comprise up to seven digits.

Publisher identifiers are assigned by the ISBN group agency responsible for the management of the ISBN system within the country, area, or language area where the publisher is officially based.

Example:

ISBN 90-70002- ...

Title Identifier

The third part of the ISBN identifies a specific edition of a publication of a specific publisher. A title identifier may consist of up to six digits. As an ISBN must always have ten digits, blank digits are represented by leading zeros.

Example:

ISBN 90-70002-04

Check Digit

The check digit is the last digit of an ISBN. ISBN 10 numbers are calculated on a modulus 11 with weights 10-2, using X in lieu of 10 where 10 would occur as a check digit.

This means that each of the first nine digits of the ISBN – excluding the check digit itself – is multiplied by a number ranging from 10 to 2, and that the resulting sum of the products, plus the check digit, must be divisible by 11 without a remainder.

Example:

ISBN 0-8436-1072-7: 978-0-9800833-0-9

Distribution of Ranges

The number of digits in each of the identifying parts 1, 2, and 3 is variable, although the total sum of digits contained in these parts is always 9. These nine digits, together with the check digit, make up the 10-digit ISBN.

The number of digits in the group identifier will vary according to the output of books in a group. Thus, groups with an expected large output will receive numbers of one or two digits and publishers with an expected large output will get numbers of two or three digits.

For ease of reading, the five parts of the ISBN are divided by spaces or hyphens.

The position of the hyphens is determined by the publisher identifier ranges that each group agency establishes in accordance with the book industry needs. The knowledge of the prefix ranges for each country or group of countries is necessary to develop the hyphenation output program.

For example, the publisher identifier ranges of group number 0 in the English language group (e.g., Australia, English-speaking Canada, Ireland, New Zealand, Puerto Rico, South Africa, Swaziland, United Kingdom, United States, and Zimbabwe) are as follows:

$$00 - 19$$
$$200 - 699$$
$$7000 - 8499$$
$$85000 - 89999$$
$$900000 - 949999$$
$$9500000 - 9999999$$

A separate ISBN must be assigned to every title or edition of a title by each publisher, but NOT to an unchanged impression or unchanged reprint of the same title in the same format by the same publisher. Revised editions require a new ISBN. A price change does not call for a new ISBN. Changes of the format induce a new ISBN. The same title published both in a series and individually is treated as two different editions.

An ISBN, once assigned, can never be reused, under any circumstances. This is of the utmost importance to avoid confusion.

If, through a clerical error, a number is incorrectly assigned, the number must be deleted from the list of useable numbers and must never be assigned to another title. Publishers should advise the group agency of the number(s) deleted and of the titles to which they were erroneously assigned.

ISBN for Software Products

An ISBN may be used to identify a specific software product. If there is more than one version (perhaps versions adapted for different machines, carrier media or language version), each version must have a separate ISBN.

When a software product is updated, revised, or amended and the changes are sufficiently substantial for the product to be called a new edition, a new ISBN must be assigned.

A relaunch of an existing product, even in new packaging, where there is no basic difference in the performance of the new and the old product, does not justify a new ISBN, and the original ISBN must be used.

When software is accompanied by a manual, which is useful only as an adjunct to the software, the software needs the manual before it can be operated, and they are sold as a package, one ISBN must be assigned to cover both items.

When two or more items in a software package can be used separately, or are sold separately as well as together, then a) the package as a whole must have an ISBN; and b) each item in the package must have an ISBN.

An ISBN should be assigned to a software product independently of its physical form (e.g., if software is available only from a remote database from where it is downloaded to the customer.)

As well as identifying the product itself, an ISBN identifies the producer or manufacturer; it should not be used to identify a distributor or wholesaler of the product.

Profiling

When profiling ISBN data, the first thing to look for is the data type. Is it a Char field? Next, confirm the assumption that the field contains the hyphen or blanks. If it is a Char field, then is it 17 characters for ISBN 13 or 13 characters for ISBN 10? This would be the only valid data type. If it is a VarChar, you may have an issue, or you may be mixing 10- and 13-character ISBN numbers in the same field. Maybe the field contains correct ISBN numbers, but some fields contain hyphens while others do not.

Alternatively, is the data type a number? The structure will vary greatly depending on the size of the publisher, so using pattern analysis will be of little help other than verifying that the data is numeric separated by spaces or hyphens. Because of the varying size of the group and publisher, it becomes difficult to use pattern analysis.

You can use the publisher to verify against a trusted source of valid publisher numbers. You can also use the check digit to verify the number. Just remember that there is a different calculation depending on the length of the number. Visit www.isbn.org as a trusted source to purchase a complete list of all ISBNs.

Social Security Number

The structure of a Social Security number is as follows:

- The first three digits denote the area where the number was issued.
- The next two digits (group numbers) are published monthly by Social Security administration.
- The final four digits are an individual number.

The group numbers range from 01 to 99. However, they are not assigned in consecutive order. For administrative reasons, group numbers are issued in the following order:

ODD numbers from 01 through 09
EVEN numbers from 10 through 98
EVEN numbers from 02 through 08
ODD numbers from 11 through 99

For example, group number 98 will be issued before 11.

Profiling

When profiling a Social Security number, first look at the inferred data type. Is it a Char, VarChar, or number? If it is a Char field, is the length 11? The length of 11 characters indicates that the data is most likely separated by special characters or spaces. If the length of the field were anything else, this indicates a potential problem. The same is true if the data type is VarChar. If the data type is a number, are all the values nine digits in length?

Next, conduct pattern analysis. Do all the values fit the same pattern (e.g., 999-99-9999 if the data type is Char 11)?

Also look at the uniqueness of the values. Are there duplicates? Should there be? If you're profiling data in a human resources system, should there be more than one employee with the same Social Security number? If these are medical records or financial services records, are there duplicates because they are multiple transactions for the same individual? When you do table analysis, does this field show up as a potential key to the table? Earlier in the book I discussed the notion of a natural key.

The Social Security number can be used to look for cross-field dependencies. Since the first three digits tell you where the number was issued, you can compare that information to such fields as place of birth. At some point United States citizens began to receive Social Security numbers at birth. Without giving away my age, I was not issued a Social Security number until I had a job and had to start paying into the Social Security system. Although I was born in New York, I was issued my Social Security number in California where I was working. So the cross-dependency rule does not apply to my Social Security number. However, since all my kids were issued a Social Security number in the hospital, the rule does apply for them. You need to be careful not to build an unbreakable rule. It seems almost ever business rule has exceptions.

The best way to validate Social Security Numbers is to subscribe to the Social Security administration's list of valid Social Security numbers.

Zone Improvement Plan (ZIP) Code

ZIP codes are the postal codes used by the United States Postal Service (USPS). Mail is supposed to be handled more efficiently and be delivered faster when ZIP codes are used (although you may debate this fact).

ZIP codes consist of five digits. An extended ZIP+4 code includes the five digits of the ZIP code, a hyphen, and then four more digits, which allow a piece of mail to be directed to a more precise location than by the ZIP code alone. ZIP+4 code identifies a geographic segment within the five-digit delivery area, such as a city block, a group of apartments, an individual high-volume receiver of mail, or any other unit requiring an extra identifier to aid in efficient mail sorting and delivery. Except for certain presorted mailings, using the ZIP+4 code is not required for mail to be delivered.

In general, mail is read by a multiline optical character reader (MOCR) that instantly determines the correct ZIP+4 code from the address and—along with the even more specific delivery point—sprays a postnet barcode on face of the mail piece that corresponds to 11 digits. This technology has greatly increased the speed and accuracy of mail delivery.

For post office boxes, the general (but not invariable) rule is that each box has its own ZIP+4 code. The add-on code is often either the last four digits of the box number or, if the box number consists of fewer than four digits, enough zeros added to the front of the box number to make it a four-digit number. However, there is no uniform rule, so the ZIP+4 code must be looked up individually for each box.

It is common to use add-on code 9998 for mail addressed to the postmaster (to which requests for pictorial cancellations are usually addressed), 9999 for general delivery, and other high-numbered add-on codes for business reply mail. For a unique ZIP code, the add-on code is typically 0001.

People who send bulk mail can get a discount on postage if they have preprinted the barcode themselves. This requires more than just a simple font; mailing lists must be standardized with up-to-date Coding Accuracy Support System (CASS) certified software that adds/verifies a full, correct ZIP+4 code and an additional two digits representing the exact delivery point.

In theory, every single mailable point in the United States has its own 11-digit number. The delivery point digits (the tenth and eleventh digits) are calculated based on the primary or secondary number of the address. The USPS publishes the rules for calculating the delivery point in a document called the CASS Technical Guide. The last digit is always a check digit, which is obtained by summing the numbers 5, 9, or 11 digits, taking the modulo base 10 of this sum (i.e., the remainder after dividing by 10) and finally subtracting this from 10. (Thus, the check digit for 10001-0001 00 would be 7, or 1+1+1=3 and 10−3=7.)

The first digit in a ZIP code represents a certain group of states. The second and third digits together represent a region in that group (or perhaps a large city), and the fourth and fifth digits represent more specific areas, such as small towns or regions of that city. The main town in a region often gets the first ZIP codes for that region; the subsequent numerical order often follows the alphabetical order of the names of town in the region.

Generally, the first three digits designate a sectional center facility, the mail sorting facility, and distribution center for an area. A sectional center facility may have more than one 3-digit code assigned to it. For example, the Northern Virginia sectional center facility in Merrifield is assigned codes 220, 221, 222 and 223.

Many of the lowest ZIP codes are in the New England region, where many begin with "0." The "0" region also include Puerto Rico, the U.S. Virgin Islands, and APO/FPO military addresses for personnel stationed in Europe. The lowest ZIP code is 00501, which is a unique ZIP Code for the U.S. Internal Revenue Service center in Holtsville, New York. Other low ZIP codes are 00969 for Guaynabo, Puerto Rico; 01001 for Agawam, Massachusetts, and 01002 for Amherst, Massachusetts.

ZIP code numbers increase southward along the East Coast, such as 02115 (Boston), 10036 (New York City), 19103 (Philadelphia), 20008 (Washington, DC), 30303 (Atlanta) and 33130 (Miami). (Each of these cities has many ZIP codes in addition to these examples.) From there, ZIP code numbers increase heading westward and northward. For example, 40202 is in Louisville, 50309 in Des Moines, Iowa, 60601 in Chicago, 75201 in Dallas, 80202 in Denver, 94111 in San Francisco, 98101 in Seattle, and 99950 in Ketchikan, Alaska.

Illustration 6.1 shows a map of U.S. ZIP code zones.

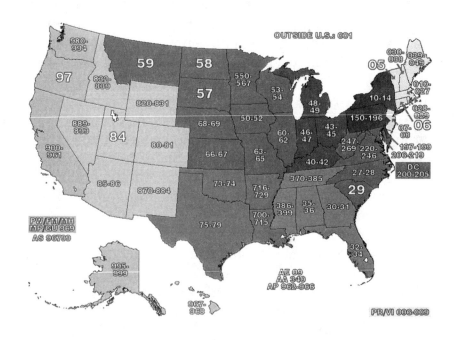

Illustration 6.1

A ZIP code's first digit represents a state:

0 = Connecticut (CT), Massachusetts (MA), Maine (ME), New Hampshire (NH), New Jersey (NJ), Puerto Rico (PR), Rhode

Island (RI), Vermont (VT), Virgin Islands (VI), APO Europe (AE), FPO Europe (AE)

1 = Delaware (DE), New York (NY), Pennsylvania (PA)

2 = District of Columbia (DC), Maryland (MD), North Carolina (NC), South Carolina (SC), Virginia (VA), West Virginia (WV)

3 = Alabama (AL), Florida (FL), Georgia (GA), Mississippi (MS), Tennessee (TN), APO Americas (AA), FPO Americas (AA)

4 = Indiana (IN), Kentucky (KY), Michigan (MI), Ohio (OH)

5 = Iowa (IA), Minnesota (MN), Montana (MT), North Dakota (ND), South Dakota (SD), Wisconsin (WI)

6 = Illinois (IL), Kansas (KS), Missouri (MO), Nebraska (NE)

7 = Arkansas (AR), Louisiana (LA), Oklahoma (OK), Texas (TX)

8 = Arizona (AZ), Colorado (CO), Idaho (ID), New Mexico (NM), Nevada (NV), Utah (UT), Wyoming (WY)

9 = Alaska (AK), American Samoa (AS), California (CA), Guam (GU), Hawaii (HI), Northern Mariana Islands (MP), Oregon (OR), Washington (WA), APO Pacific (AP), FPO Pacific (AP)

Other U.S. territories have codes starting with 9. However, with the expansion of ZIP codes, the first digit is not always assigned to a group of states. For example, in New York ZIP codes begin with 0 and 1; in the District of Columbia they begin with 2 and 5; in Texas they begin with 7 and 8.

The next two digits represent the sectional center facility (e.g., 432xx = Columbus, OH). The fourth and fifth digits represent the area of the city (if in a metropolitan area), or a village/town (outside metro areas). For example, for the ZIP code 43209, 4 = Ohio, 32 = Columbus, 09 = Bexley. When a sectional center facility's area crosses state lines, that facility is assigned separate three-digit prefixes for the states that it serves; thus, it is possible to identify the state associated with any ZIP code just by looking at the first three digits. Often, the last two digits are assigned in alphabetical order to each community for sorting centers that serve multiple cities.

It is important to note that despite the geographic derivation of most ZIP codes, the codes themselves are not geographic regions, but simply categories for grouping mailing addresses. ZIP code "areas" can overlap, be subsets of each other, or be artificial constructs with no geographic area. Similarly, in areas without regular postal routes (rural route areas) or no mail delivery (undeveloped areas), ZIP codes are not assigned or are based on sparse delivery routes, and hence the boundary between ZIP code areas is undefined.

For example, federal government agencies in and around the nation's capital are assigned ZIP codes starting with 20200 to 20599, which are Washington, DC ZIP codes, even if they are not located in Washington DC itself. While the White House itself is located in ZIP code 20006, it has the ZIP code 20500. The Nuclear Regulatory Commission is located in Rockville, Maryland, at ZIP code 20852, but the Postal Service has assigned it a Washington, DC 20555 address. Similarly, the United States Patent and Trademark Office used to be located in Crystal City, Virginia at ZIP code 22202, but it was assigned the address Washington, DC 20231, Since this its move to Alexandria, Virginia, however, the Patent and Trademark Office now uses the ZIP+4 code 22313-1450.

Rarely is a locality assigned a ZIP code that does not match the rest of the state. However, when the locality is so isolated that it is served from a sectional center in another state, it is assigned a different ZIP code. For example, Fishers Island, New York, bears the ZIP code 06390 and is served from Connecticut. All other New York ZIP codes (except those at Holtsville for the IRS) begin with "1."

ZIP Codes Only Loosely Tied to Cities

When an address's ZIP code and the city name appear on the same line, it doesn't necessarily mean that that address is within that city. The Postal Service designates a single "default" place name for each ZIP code. This may be an actual incorporated town or city, a sub entity of a town or city, or an unincorporated U.S. Census-designated place. Other additional place names may also be recognized as "acceptable" for a certain ZIP code. Still others are deemed "not acceptable," and if used may result in a delay in mail delivery.

Default place names are typically the actual city or town in which the address is located. However, for many cities that have incorporated since ZIP codes were introduced, the actual city name is only "acceptable" and not the default place name. Many databases automatically assign the default place name for a ZIP code without regard to any "acceptable" place names. For example, Centennial, Colorado, the largest city to incorporate in U.S. history, is divided among seven ZIP codes assigned to Aurora, Englewood, or Littleton as its default place names. Thus, postally speaking, the city of Centennial and its 100,000 residents do not exist—they are part of Aurora, Englewood, or Littleton. In the ZIP code directory, Centennial addresses are listed under those three cities. And since it is acceptable to write Centennial in conjunction with any of the seven ZIP codes, one can write Centennial in an address that is actually in Aurora, Englewood, or Littleton, as long as it is in one of the shared ZIP codes.

Acceptable place names are often added to a ZIP code in cases where the ZIP code boundaries divide them into two or more cities, as in the case of Centennial. However, in many cases only the default name can be used, even when many addresses in the ZIP code are in another city. For example, approximately 85 percent of the area served by the ZIP code 85254, to which the place name Scottsdale, Arizona is assigned, is actually inside the city limits of neighboring Phoenix. This is because the post office that serves this area is in Scottsdale. This has led some residents of the ZIP code to believe that they live in Scottsdale when they actually live in Phoenix. A City of Scottsdale Web site states that the 85254 ZIP code is considered to a positive aspect of the city because the name "Scottsdale" is used for businesses located outside the city limits in Phoenix.

This phenomenon occurs across the country. Englewood, Colorado is a land-locked, inner-ring suburb that was built out by the 1960s. Its post office served the area that is now the high-growth southern tier of the Denver metropolitan area, and ZIP codes in this area were assigned Englewood as their default place name. An employment center as large as downtown Denver has grown in this area, and its office parks are the headquarters for many internationally recognized corporations. Even though they are actually located in other cities, they indicate Englewood as their location, as this is the default postal place name. As a result, there are really two Englewoods—the actual city, small and with a largely working class residential population, and, a number of miles away, the postal Englewood, a vast suburban area of up-scale subdivisions and office parks that have nothing to do with the city of Englewood. The identity of Englewood is split due to its assigned ZIP codes. People who say that they live or work in Englewood and identify closely with it may rarely enter the actual city of that name.

Acceptable place names also come into play in areas of the country where many citizens identify more strongly with a particular urban center than the municipality in which they actually reside. For example, Allegheny County, Pennsylvania has 130 distinct municipalities, but many of the county's residents, and even some residents of adjacent counties, commonly use Pittsburgh, PA as their postal address.

Finally, many ZIP codes are for villages, U.S. Census-designated places, portions of cities, or other entities that are not municipalities. For example, ZIP code 03750 is for Etna, New Hampshire, but Etna is not a city or town; it is actually a village district in the town of Hanover, which itself is assigned the ZIP code 03755. Another example is ZIP code 08043, which corresponds to Kirkwood, New Jersey but actually serves the entirety of Voorhees Township, New Jersey.

The postal designations for place names become *de facto* locations for their addresses, and as a result, it is difficult to convince residents and businesses that they actually are located in another city or town. Because this situation causes both geographic and cultural confusion, some cities, such as Signal Hill, California, have successfully petitioned the Postal Service to change ZIP code boundaries or create new ZIP codes so that their cities can be the default place name for addresses within the ZIP code.

This confusion also can have financial implications for local governments, because mail volume is among the factors used by the U.S. Census to estimate population changes between decennial census enumerations. Sometimes local officials advise residents of community (not the default place name for a ZIP code, but an acceptable place name) to always use the name of the community to avoid inaccurate population counts, which negatively affect the amount of state and federal government funding the community receives.

Division and Reallocation of ZIP Codes

Like area codes, ZIP codes are sometimes divided and changed, especially when a rural area becomes suburban. Typically, the new codes become effective once announced, and a grace period (e.g., one year) is provided in which the new and old codes are used concurrently so that postal patrons in the affected area can notify correspondents, order new stationery, etc.

Most significantly, in rapidly developing suburbs it is sometimes necessary to open a new sectional center facility, which must then be allocated its own three-digit ZIP code prefix or prefixes. Such allocation can be done in various ways. For example, when a new sectional center facility was opened at Dulles Airport in Virginia, the prefix 201 was allocated to that facility; therefore, for all post offices to be served by that sectional center facility, the ZIP code changed from an old code beginning with 220 or 221 to a new code or codes beginning with 201. However, when a new sectional center facility was opened to serve Montgomery County, Maryland, no new prefix was assigned. Instead, ZIP codes in the 207 and 208 ranges, which had previously been assigned alphabetically, were reshuffled so that 207xx ZIP codes in the county were changed to 208xx codes, while 208xx codes outside that county were changed to 207xx codes. Because Silver Spring (whose postal area includes Wheaton) has its own prefix, 209, there was no need to apply the reshuffling to Silver Spring; instead, all mail going to 209xx ZIP codes was simply rerouted to the new sectional center facility.

ZIP codes also change when postal boundaries are realigned. For example, when the change in Montgomery County took place, and under pressure from then-mayor of Washington DC, Marion Barry, the USPS realigned the postal boundaries between the District of Columbia and Maryland to match the actual boundary. Previously, many inner suburbs, such as Bethesda and Tacoma Park, had been in the Washington DC postal area. As a result of the change, ZIP codes in Maryland beginning with 200 were changed to new ZIP codes beginning with 207, 208, or 209, depending on their location, and ZIP codes straddling the DC–Maryland line were split. For example, 20014 (Bethesda) became 20814, while the Maryland portion of 20012 (Tacoma Park) became 20912.

By Type/Use

There are three types of ZIP codes: 1) unique, assigned to a single high-volume mailer; 2) P.O. box-only, used only for P.O. boxes at a given facility and not for any other type of delivery; and 3) standard, assigned to all other ZIP codes. As examples of unique ZIP codes, certain governmental agencies, universities, businesses, or buildings that receive extremely high volumes of mail have their own ZIP codes, such as 81009 for the Federal Citizen Information Center of the US General Services Administration (GSA) in Pueblo, Colorado; 15705 for Indiana University of Pennsylvania in Indiana, Pennsylvania; 92803 for Disneyland in California, and 32830 for Walt Disney World in Florida; 30385 for BellSouth in Atlanta; 12345 for General Electric in Schenectady, New York; 10048 for the World Trade Center complex in New York, New York (until its destruction on September 11, 2001), and 77230 for victims of Hurricane Katrina being housed at the Houston Astrodome. The White House has its own secret ZIP+4 code, separate from the publicly known 20500, for the President of the United States and the first family to receive private mail. An example of a P.O. box-only ZIP code is 22313, which is used for P.O. boxes at the main post office in Alexandria, Virginia. In the area surrounding that post office, home and business mail delivery addresses use ZIP code 22314, which is thus a standard ZIP code.

To make this clearer, let's look at the allocation of ZIP codes in Princeton, New Jersey:

- 08540—standard (deliveries in most of the Princeton postal area)
- 08541—unique (Educational Testing Service)
- 08542—standard (deliveries in the central area of the borough of Princeton, and also some P.O. boxes)
- 08543—P.O. box only (P.O. boxes at the main post office)
- 08544—unique (Princeton University)

Another unique type of ZIP code is M—military 34036, Military—Armed Forces Americas (except Canada).

Other Uses

Delivery services other than the USPS, such as FedEx, United Parcel Service, and DHL, require a ZIP code for optimal internal routing of a package. This spares customers from being required to use some other routing designator, such as the International Air Transport Association (IATA) code of the destination airport or railhead.

ZIP codes are used not only for tracking of mail but in gathering geographical statistics in the United States. The U.S. Census Bureau keeps track of the latitude and longitude of the center point of each ZIP code, a database that numerous other companies sell. The data are often used in direct mail campaigns in a process called ZIP code marketing, developed by Martin Baier. Point-of-sale cashiers sometimes ask consumers what ZIP code they live in to collect corporate purchasing-pattern data. The corporation or specialists then analyze these data to determine the location of new business establishments. Finally, ZIP coded data are also used in analyzing geographic factors in risk, an insurance industry and banking practice negatively known as redlining.

Profiling

Leave it to the government to create rules and then break them at every turn. When profiling ZIP code data, as usual start with data type. Is it inferred to be a number, character, or VarChar? If the data type is inferred as character and the data is correct, this means that there are separators included in the data like a hyphen. A number means there are no separators. A VarChar might mean that some values are a ZIP code and others are ZIP+4.

Next, look at the length to see if it is 5, 9, 10, or some other value. If all the values are numbers and are five digits in length, then you are dealing with ZIP codes only. If all the values are nine or ten digits in length, then you are dealing with ZIP +4. If the data contains characters, then either the data is bad, or you are dealing with international addresses.

The next step is pattern analysis. If the values are numeric and are five or nine digits long, do a quick check to make sure they are all that length. You should see a pattern of 9(5) or 9(9). Anything else would be invalid. If the field is inferred to be a Char or VarChar, look for patterns like:

9(5) –9(4)
9(5)
9(9)

What if you see a pattern like 9(5)-999? It could be wrong, or you could have some Brazilian ZIP codes. Hopefully you've followed my advice and have sorted by the number of unique values. When you were profiling the data, you should have passed the country code before you got to the ZIP code. Therefore, you would know if you are dealing with an international address before you get to the postal code field.

Are there nulls in the ZIP code? We know that every mailable address in the United States requires a ZIP code. I have had mail returned by the USPS because it did not have a ZIP code, although it had a complete and accurate address.

A potential, although not hard and fast business rule is whether the ZIP+4 matches the P.O. box. Do any of your ZIP codes include special ZIP codes like the IRS processing center on Long Island? Even if you do business with the IRS, this is not the ZIP code you send invoices to.

Does your ZIP code field also contain postcodes for Canada? Europe? These would show up as Char or VarChar and the patterns would be different.

Remember: valid ZIP codes change over time. Tables allow you to validate ZIP code to state, but again, this is not a hard and fast rule because some ZIP codes cross state bounders. ZIP code to county has the same problem, and ZIP code to metro area is not well behaved.

Is the minimum value greater than 00501?

There are many address validation programs available that cleanse address data, but when profiling the data, you are trying to assess the data's current state.

ELECTRONIC PRODUCT CODE (EPC)

The EPC, is a family of coding schemes for radio-frequency identification (RFID) tags. These schemes are designed to meet the needs of various industries, while guaranteeing uniqueness for all EPC-compliant tags. The EPC accommodates existing coding schemes and defines new schemes where necessary.

The EPC was the creation of the MIT Auto-ID Center, a consortium of over 120 global corporations and university labs. The EPC system is currently managed by EPCglobal, Inc., a subsidiary of GS1, creators of the Universal Product Code (UPC) barcode.

The EPC promises to become the standard for global RFID usage, and is a core element of the proposed EPCglobal Network.

All EPC numbers contain a header that identifies the encoding scheme that has been used. The header in turn dictates the length, type, and structure of the EPC. EPC encoding schemes frequently contain a serial number that can be used to uniquely identify one object.

While I have not had any experience profiling EPC data, I mention it here because you will begin seeing EPC data in the near future.

CREDIT CARD NUMBER

Specifications for credit card numbering have been drawn up by the International Standards Organization (ISO/IEC 7812-1:1993) and the American National Standards Institute (ANSI X4.13)

Major Industry Identifier

MII Digit Value	Issuer Category
0	ISO/TC 68 and other industry assignments
1	Airlines
2	Airlines and other industry assignments
3	Travel and entertainment
4	Banking and financial
5	Banking and financial
6	Merchandizing and banking
7	Petroleum
8	Telecommunications and other industry assignments
9	National assignment

Table 6.8

The **first digit** of your credit card number is the major industry identifier (MII), which represents the category of entity that issued your credit card. Different MII digits represent the following issuer categories, as illustrated in Table 6.8.

For example, American Express, Diner's Club, and Carte Blanche are in the travel and entertainment category; VISA, MasterCard, and Discover are in the banking and financial category; and SUN Oil and Exxon are in the petroleum category.

Issuer Identifier

The first six digits of your credit card number (including the initial MII digit) form the issuer identifier.

Some of the better known issuer identifiers are listed in owing Table 6.9.

Issuer	Identifier	Card Number Length
Diner's Club / Carte Blanche	300xxx-305xxx, 36xxxx, 38xxxx	14
American Express	34xxxx, 37xxxx	15
VISA	4xxxxx	13, 16
MasterCard	51xxxx-55xxxx	16
Discover	6011xx	16

Table 6.9

If the MII digit is 9, then the next three digits of the issuer identifier are the three-digit country codes defined in ISO 3166, and the remaining final two digits of the issuer identifier can be defined by the national standards body of the specified country in whatever way it wishes.

Account Number

Digits 7 to (n–1) of your credit card number are your individual account identifier. The maximum length of a credit card number is 19 digits.

Check Digit

The final digit of your credit card number is a check digit. The algorithm used to arrive at the proper check digit is called the Luhn algorithm, named after IBM scientist Hans Peter Luhn. When dealing with credit cards it is important to realize that some have different lengths and have different prefixes, as noted earlier.

All of these credit cards use (mod 10) to determine a check digit, and in all cases, the check digit is the right-most digit in the number. To determine the check digit for a credit card follow these steps:

NOTE: MasterCard and VISA include the prefix digits in the calculation. With American Express and Discover, the prefix digits are omitted from all calculations.

NOTE: For the following example we consider a random possible MasterCard number 5368235896831135.

Step 1: Starting from the second digit from the right and moving towards the left, multiply every digit by 2.

$3*2 = 6$
$1*2 = 2$
$8*2 = 16$
$9*2 = 18$
$5*2 = 10$
$2*2 = 4$
$6*2 = 12$
$5*2 = 10$

Step 2: Sum the digits from Step 1.

$6 + 2 + 1 + 6 + 1 + 8 + 1 + 0 + 4 + 1 + 2 + 1 + 0 = 33$

Step 3: Sum all of the digits not originally multiplied by 2.

$3 + 8 + 3 + 8 + 6 + 3 + 1 = 32$

Step 4: Sum together the results from Step 2 and Step 3.

$33 + 32 = 55$

Step 5: Subtract the sum from the next highest multiple of 10.

60 -55 = 5 [check digit]

A person can determine if the check digit of a given credit card is valid by repeating Steps 1, 2, 3, 4 for all digits, including the check digit. The sum, s, obtained in Step 4 should be $s = 0 \pmod{10}$. In this case, $60 = 0 \pmod{10}$.

The following are credit cards numbers in a valid format:

American Express	3400 0000 0000 009
Carte Blanche	3000 0000 0000 04
Discover	6011 0000 0000 0004
Diner's Club	3000 0000 0000 04
enRoute	2014 0000 0000 009
JCB	2131 0000 0000 0008
MasterCard	5500 0000 0000 0004
Solo	6334 0000 0000 0004
Switch	4903 0100 0000 0009
VISA	4111 1111 1111 1111

Profiling

When profiling credit card data, start with data type. Is it a number or VarChar? If it is a number, you can assume there are no separators. If it is VarChar, you can assume there are separators, but I would use patterns to confirm this assumption. If the data type is Char, see if there are leading or trailing blanks to fill up to 16 characters. Another possibility may be that your data represents only one credit card. Maybe the business only accepts American Express.

The length of the credit card number (i.e., American Express = 15, Diners Club = 14, Discover = 16, Master Card = 14 or 16, and VISA = 13 or 16) indicates that all credit card types are accepted, or that you have issues with the data. Pattern analysis reveals these issues quickly and gives you some indications on which cards are accepted.

The credit card number's prefix (i.e., American Express 34 or 37, Diners Club 300–305, 36, 38, Discover 6011 and 650, Master Card 51–55, 36 VISA 4) can be used to validate other information contained in the record, like card type and percent payable to vendor.

A further breakdown of the structure of an American Express card number looks like this:

1–4 = country code, currency code, and type (i.e., charge or credit)

5-6 = card type (e.g., gold, platinum)

7 = billing cycle

8-11 = account number

card issue (if replaced)

card number (multimember)

last digit check digit

Again, you can use country code in the card to validate against country code in the record. I am not sure how to determine the currency code, unless American Express issues cards in only a few currencies. In addition, charge type can be used to determine that if it is a charge card, there should not be an interest percentage number in that field.

You can also use the check digit calculation to validate a card number.

In addition, on the back of your card there is an additional credit card code. This is three digits, but American Express cards use four.

While credit card vendors could provide you with a valid list of numbers, that list changes every second.

Oil Well Identifiers

American Petroleum Institute (API)

The API number is a number the American Petroleum Institute uses to identify oil and gas wells throughout the U.S. The number is fourteen digits and is broken into five parts.

Here is an example of the API numbering structure: 42-501-20130-03-00

State Code

The first two digits of the API number represent the surface location of the state in which the well is located. In this example, the surface location of this well is located in state code 42 or Texas. Keep in mind that the bottom hole location of this well may be in a contiguous state such as Louisiana, Oklahoma, or New Mexico, but the API number is based on the surface location. This differs from the Canadian Unique Well Identifier (UWI), which identifies the bottom hole location. Please refer to an API State Code List in the appendix for a complete listing of state and pseudo state codes. Since not all wells are drilled on land, additional codes needed to be added to the list. For example, code 61 refers to Atlantic Coast Offshore.

County Code

The third through fifth digits of the API number represent the surface location of the county where the well is located. In this example, the well is located in county code 501 or Yoakum County. Again, keep in mind that the bottom hole location may be in a contiguous county, but the API number is based on the surface location.

Please note that all county codes are odd numbers except for certain counties in Arizona and New Mexico and Kern County, California. This was designed for expansion. Kern County's well population has exceeded 99,999, so 029 is used for the first 99,999 wells and 030 for the wells drilled after that.

County codes are also used to designate offshore areas for both state and federal waters.

Unique Well Identifier

In most states, the sixth through tenth digit of the API number is assigned as a unique number within the county the well is drilled. In a few states, the unique well identifier is based on the permit number and may only be unique within the state.

In most cases, the series 00000 has been used for historical wells (i.e., wells drilled prior to the issuance of API numbers). The series 10000–50000 are used by most states for current numbers.

Directional Sidetrack Code

The sidetrack code is the eleventh and twelfth digits of the API number. It is used to identify each sidetrack uniquely for the well. A good rule of thumb is to increment the sidetrack code for each unique bottom hole location of the well. In the aforementioned example, this is the third sidetrack off the original well bore.

Event Sequence Code

The thirteenth and fourteenth digits of the API number indicate how many operations there have been on a single borehole. It is incremented only when part of the borehole identified in the eleventh and twelfth positions is deepened, recompleted, or worked over. Since the aforementioned example shows a code of 00, we know that this is the original drill of sidetrack #3, even though the original and either or both of the previous sidetracks may have been recompleted. (It is important to remember that this code may vary between data vendors based on their database recompletion criteria.)

Canadian Unique Well Identifier (UWI)

The Canadian UWI is the standard 16-character code, which defines the bottom hole location and each significant drilling or completion event in the well.

UWI in the Dominion Land Survey (DLS) System

Example well location 14-36-85-17 W6
UWI 100 14 36 085 17 W6 00

Character	1	2	3	4,5	6,7	8-10	11,12	13,14	15	16
UWI	1	0	0	14	36	085	17	W6	0	0
Desc				LSD	Sect	Town	Range	Meridian		Event

In the DLS system, the first character is always "1."

The second character is always "0" (zero).

The third character indicates the chronological sequence of wells drilled in the legal subdivision (LSD):

"0" denotes the first well,
"2" denotes the second well,
"3" the third, etc.
For example, if the UWI is 1 02 14 36 085 17 W6 00,

"2" indicates that this is the second well drilled to a bottom hole location in LSD 14.

For a vertical hole, the corresponding surface location is written A14-36-85-17.

The fourth and fifth characters identify the LSD.

The sixth and seventh characters identify the section.

The eighth, ninth and tenth characters identify the township.

The eleventh and twelfth characters identify the range.

The thirteenth and fourteenth characters identify
the meridian
All wells in northeast British Columbia are west of the 6th meridian (W6). The fifteenth character is always "0" (zero).

The sixteenth character, the event sequence code, indicates the significant drilling and/or completion operations at a well which yield a separate and unique set of geological or production data. The initial drilling and firstcompletion are coded "0" (zero) and subsequent events 2–9. (Event sequence code 1 is not used). An event sequence code other than zero is created because of:

- deepening a well
- re-entry of a well
- whipstocked portion of a well
- second and subsequent completions

UWI in the National Topographic System (NTS)

Example well location d-96-H/94-A-15
UWI 200 D 096 H 094A15 00

Character	1	2	3	4	5-7	8	9-14	15	16
UWI	2	0	0	d	096	H	094A15	0	0
Description				¼ Unit	Unit	Block	NTS Map Sheet		Event

In the NTS system the first character is always "2."

The second character is always "0" (zero).

The third character indicates the chronological sequence of wells drilled in the Quarter Unit:

"0" denotes the first well,
"2" denotes the second well,
"3" the third, etc.

For example, if the UWI is 2 03 D 096 H 094 A 15 00, the "3" indicates that this is the third well drilled to a bottom hole location in 1/4 unit "d".
For a vertical hole, the corresponding surface location is written d-B96-H/94-A-15.

The fourth character identifies the quarter unit.
The fifth to seventh characters identify the unit.
The eighth character identifies the block.
The ninth to fourteenth characters identify the NTS map sheet number.
The fifteenth character is always "0" (zero).

The sixteenth character, the event sequence code, indicates the significant drilling and/or completion operations at a well which yield a separate and unique set of geological or production data. See the description in the DLS well example.

Note: There is a group that is trying to create a Global Unique Well Identifier (GUWI) for wells outside of North America, but adoption has been slow.

Profiling

When profiling oil well data, start with the data type. Is it inferred to be an integer? The API number is usually not stored with separators. Then look at the length of the field. Is it 14 digits? If there are 14 digits, then you are only dealing with U.S. wells. Use pattern analysis to make sure all the values are a specific length and to identify the Canadian UWI.

One technique I have used on U.S. well data identifiers is to strip off the state and county parts and validate them using reference data. In addition, if there is other location data contained in the record, can you do cross field validation?

PHONE NUMBER

The North American Numbering Plan (NANP) is an integrated telephone-numbering plan serving 19 North American countries that share its resources. These countries include the United States and its territories, Canada, Bermuda, Anguilla, Antigua and Barbuda, the Bahamas, Barbados, the British Virgin Islands, the Cayman Islands, Dominica, the Dominican Republic, Grenada, Jamaica, Montserrat, St. Kitts and Nevis, St. Lucia, St. Vincent and the Grenadines, Trinidad and Tobago, and Turks and Caicos.

The structure of the North American phone number is as follows:

Numbering Plan Area (NPA) (a.k.a. area code) = [2–9][0–8][0–9]
Nxx = [2–9][0–9][0–9] Station = [0–9][0–9][0–9][0–9]

The first value cannot be a 1 because that is what triggers long distance and routing the call to your long distance carrier. Here's a interesting tidbit: the reason you do not have to dial a 1 when you use your cell phone is because the entire long distance part of the call is handled by the cell phone company and therefore does not need to be routed anywhere but within the cell phone company.

The values N11 in the area code are reserved for service codes, for example, 411 for information and 911 for emergencies. The values 37X and 96X reserved for unanticipated purposes

Profiling

When profiling phone numbers, first look at the data type. Has it been inferred as a number? If so, there are no special characters involved. Has it been inferred as a Char? If so, it is fixed length and includes special characters or letters. Has it been inferred as a VarChar? Then it has special characters or letters and is not a standard value. This is the worst of the three because you have no standard representation of a phone number.

Next, look at the length—is it a variable length or are all the entries a standard length? Standard is better. If the length were ten, then I would assume it would include the area code and phone number. If the length were eleven, then I would check to see if the 1 is included in a North American number or if it is a European phone number. If the number were seven digits long, I would think the phone number did not include the area code. Many times, the area code is in a separate field.

Next, look at the patterns in the data. Here are a number of patterns that may exist within a phone field:

Patterns	Matching	Frequency
p999qb999-9999	1706	14.96%

This represents a number that looks like (201) 734-2222.

Patterns	Matching	Frequency
99bp99qb9999b9999	169	1.48%

This represents a number that looks like 61 (03) 9655 7131, an Australian phone number.

Patterns	Matching	Frequency
9(11)	152	1.33%

This represents a number is a European phone number (e.g., Moscow, Spain, etc.), without any special formatting characters or a U.S. number with the 1 included for long distance dialing.

Patterns	Matching	Frequency
9.9(5)U+99	142	1.24%

This example shows values that were converted by Microsoft® Excel® or some other program to numeric notation.

Patterns	Matching	Frequency
99/999/9(6)	96	0.84%

This probably represents a number is a European phone number (e.g., Germany, Netherlands, Italy, etc.) with country code/area code/number.

Pattern	Matching	Frequency
99/9/9(8)	92	0.80%
99/99/9(7)	90	0.78%
+99b9(9)	86	0.75%
+99b99b999b99b99	86	0.75%
-9(6)	85	0.74%
+99b9b99b99b99b99	80	0.70%

9(10)	53	0.46%
+99b9999b9(6)	51	0.44%
+99b999b9(6)	41	0.35%
-9(5)	41	0.35%
-9(9)	41	0.35%
999/9/9(7	41	0.35%
+99b99b99b99b99	40	0.35%
+99b999b999b999	36	0.31%
999/9(6)	34	0.29%
99/9(9)	30	0.26%
+99b99b99b999b999	28	0.24%
C(40)	24	0.21%

I did not bother to look at the validity of these other patterns. Although this pattern C(40) is particularly interesting, it contains values like: Esther 401-329-3156/Comfort 401-329-8352

Pattern	Matching	Frequency
99b9b99b99b99b99	23	0.20%
+99b9(8)	21	0.18%
+99b999b999b99b99	20	0.17%
-9(8)	15	0.13%
99/9(7)	14	0.12%
999/99/9(6)	14	0.12%
999/99/9(7)	13	0.11%
999/999/9(6)	12	0.10%

You can see that pattern analysis helps ferret out the issues with a phone number pretty quickly. While viewing the values and sorting them alphabetically will show you issues, patterns show you how bad the problem is.

I like to use valid values to help identify potential problems. The easiest would be to compare the area code to an area code table. An area code table is included in the appendix of this book. Using this data it is easy to perform a validation of area codes. Using one profiling product, I can import the table and validate values against the domain set. I can also bring in the reference table like any other table and do cross-table analysis with this table to come up with values that are not included in the reference table. I can also build a join and show nonoverlapping values. I can use many different techniques to get the answer I am looking for.

I can also purchase data that contains area code and valid exchanges within those area codes. This allows me to validate all the area codes and local exchanges within the area codes.

There are companies that allow you to validate area codes and exchanges against states and cities or ZIP codes, which helps you compare the area code to address data. You can be validating address data or phone number or both.

You can use the information in Table 6.10 to validate area code, exchange, city, state, and type of phone number (cell phone vs. landline). This table is for New Jersey. Given an address and phone number, you can validate the area code depending on the state, the exchange based upon the area code and/or city, or whether the phone is a residence or business phone number or a cell phone number.

As always, be careful of the rules. When I lived in New Jersey, I had an area code of 732. My next-door neighbor had an area code of 609. We had a special tariff that allow us to make calls to several area codes without using (and being charged) long distance.

Area Code	Prefix	City/Switch Name	Telephone Company	Telco Type
201	200	JERSEY CITY	VERIZON NEW JERSEY, INC.	RBOC
201	201	XXXXXXXXXX	VERIZON NEW JERSEY, INC.	RBOC
201	202	HACKENSACK	ARCH WIRELESS HOLDINGS, INC.	WIRELESS PROV
201	204	JERSEY CITY	METROCALL	WIRELESS PROV
201	206	HACKENSACK	NEXTEL COMMUNICATIONS	WIRELESS PROV
201	207	NEWARK	CELLCO PARTNERSHIP DBA VERIZON WIRELESS - NJ	WIRELESS PROV
201	208	NEWARK	WINSTAR OF NEW JERSEY, LLC - NJ	CLEC
201	209	JERSEY CITY	VERIZON NEW JERSEY, INC.	RBOC
201	210	NEWARK	AT&T LOCAL	CLEC
201	211	XXXXXXXXXX	VERIZON NEW JERSEY, INC.	RBOC
201	212	LEONIA	SCOTT SABO DBA ALLPAGE	WIRELESS PROV
201	213	MORRISTOWN	CELLCO PARTNERSHIP DBA VERIZON WIRELESS - NJ	WIRELESS PROV
201	214	HACKENSACK	AT&T WIRELESS SERVICES, INC.	WIRELESS PROV
201	215	ELIZABETH	PAETEC COMMUNICATIONS, INC. - NJ	CLEC

201	216	JERSEY CITY	VERIZON NEW JERSEY, INC.	RBOC
201	217	JERSEY CITY	VERIZON NEW JERSEY, INC.	RBOC
201	218	HACKENSACK	AT&T WIRELESS SERVICES, INC.	WIRELESS PROV
201	219	JERSEY CITY	ARCH WIRELESS HOLDINGS, INC.	WIRELESS PROV
201	220	HACKENSACK	AT&T WIRELESS SERVICES, INC.	WIRELESS PROV
201	221	ROCHELLE PARK	TELEPORT COMMUNICATIONS GROUP - NEW YORK - NJ	CAP
201	222	JERSEY CITY	VERIZON NEW JERSEY, INC.	RBOC
201	223	UNION CITY	VERIZON NEW JERSEY, INC.	RBOC
201	224	LEONIA	VERIZON NEW JERSEY, INC.	RBOC
201	225	ORADELL	VERIZON NEW JERSEY, INC.	RBOC
201	226	ROCHELLE PARK	VERIZON NEW JERSEY, INC.	RBOC
201	227	ENGLEWOOD	VERIZON NEW JERSEY, INC.	RBOC
201	228	BERGEN	AT&T LOCAL	CLEC
201	229	LITTLE FERRY	VERIZON NEW JERSEY, INC.	RBOC

Table 6.10

There are also companies that validate phone numbers in real time at the point of entry, or you can use the tables in the appendix. Alternatively, you may contact you local phone company to see if it can provide you with valid local phone number lists.

FINANCIAL SERVICES NUMBERS

A **Committee on Uniform Security Identification Procedures (CUSIP)** number is a unique, nine-character, alphanumeric identifier that is permanently assigned to a specific security issuer and its issues, offered in North America.

The first six characters identify the issuer and are assigned to issuers in alphabetic sequence. The next two characters identify the issue; these can be alphabetic or numeric to differentiate between fixed income instruments and equity securities. The ninth character is a check digit used to mathematically verify the accuracy of the number during data transmission. Here is an example:

CUSIP: 392690QT3

An **International Securities Identification Number (ISIN)** is a 12-character global securities identification standard created by the International Organization for Standardization (ISO), used by National Numbering Agencies (NNA) to identify international securities. The ISIN standard is codified as ISO 6166. ISINs consist of a two-character country code, followed by a nine-character local identifier (such as CUSIP/CINS), followed by a one-character check digit. A significant percentage of global ISINs are constructed from the underlying nine-character CUSIP and/or CINS code. Here is an example:

ISIN: CH0001998233

CUSIP International Numbering System (CINS) numbers are nine-character alphanumeric identifiers assigned to non-North American securities. They employ the same nine characters as CUSIP numbers, but CINS numbers are characterized by an alpha in the first position signifying the issuer's country or geographic region. CINS were developed as an extension to the CUSIP system in 1989, in response to U.S. demand for global coverage within a nine-character structure. Here is an example:

CINS: G0052B105

A CSB-ISIN is An ISIN number derived from a CUSIP or CINS number issued by the CUSIP Service Bureau (CSB). For instruments within the jurisdiction of the CUSIP Service Bureau, the ISIN number is created by taking a nine-digit CUSIP or CINS Number, adding a two-digit ISO country prefix to the beginning of the CUSIP/CINS (positions 1–2), and then add a computer-generated check digit to the end (position 12). A CSB ISIN will always contain the CUSIP or CINS number in positions 3–11. The conversion of CUSIP numbers into the 12-digit ISIN satisfies the ISIN number structure specified in ISO 6166. Here is an example:

CSB ISIN: US4592001024

Committee on Uniform Security Identification Procedures (CUSIP)

A CUSIP number identifies most securities, including stocks of all registered U.S. and Canadian companies, and U.S. government and municipal bonds. The CUSIP system – owned by the American Bankers Association and operated by Standard & Poor's – facilitates the clearing and settlement process of securities.

The number consists of nine characters (including letters and numbers) that uniquely identify a company or issuer and the type of security. A similar system is used to identify foreign securities (CUSIP international numbering system).

The first six characters of the CUSIP nine-digit alphanumeric security identifier are known as the base, which uniquely identifies the issuer of the instrument. The last two characters of the issuer code can be letters. The numbers from 990000 up are reserved, as are xxx990 and up within each group of 1000 (i.e., 100990 to 1009ZZ).

The seventh and eighth digits identify the exact issue, numbers for equity and letters for fixed income. The ninth digit is an automatically generated check digit. The check digit is calculated using modulus ten.

Profiling

When profiling a CUSIP number, the first thing to look at is the data type. Is it a Char value? If it is inferred as a VarChar, you know you have some issues. Since a CUSIP is a nine-character value, all CUSIPs should be inferred as a Char value.

Next, look at the length of the field. Again, it should only be nine positions in length. Anything longer or shorter is incorrect. Use patterns, but only to look for special characters, blanks, etc.

Also look at uniqueness. If this is a transaction system or an inventory system where you can have multiple transactions in the same security, you should not be concerned. If this is a reference table where you should only have one entry for each security, then be concerned.

Another way to validate a CUSIP number is to calculate the check digit for the number and compare it to the check digit associated with the number in your data. This verifies if you have a valid CUSIP number, not necessarily correct for this instrument.

The best way to validate a CUSIP number is to use a trusted source. You can purchase a list of financial instruments that include the valid CUSIP number and a description of the instrument.

(International Securities Identification Number) ISIN

ISINs consist of three parts: a two-letter country code, a nine-character alphanumeric national security identifier, and a single check digit. The country code is the ISO alpha-2 code for the country of issue, which is not necessarily the country in which the issuing company is domiciled. International securities cleared through Clearstream or Euroclear, which are Europe-wide, use XS as the country code.

The nine-digit security identifier is the National Securities Identifying Number, or NSIN, assigned by governing bodies in each country, known as the national numbering agency (NNA). In North America the NNA is the CUSIP organization, meaning that CUSIPs can easily be converted into ISINs by adding the U.S. or Canada country code to the beginning of the existing CUSIP code and adding an additional check digit at the end. For example, Apple Computer: ISIN US0378331005, expanded from CUSIP 037833100.

In England and Ireland, the NNA is the London Stock Exchange, and the NSIN is the Stock Exchange Daily Official List (SEDOL), converted in a similar fashion after padding the SEDOL number out with leading zeros. Most other countries use similar conversions, but if no country NNA exists regional NNAs are used instead.

ISIN check digits are based on the same Modulus 10 Double Add Double technique used in CUSIPs. To calculate the check digit every second digit is multiplied by two. Letters are converted to numbers by adding their ordinal position in the alphabet to 9, such that A = 10 and M = 22. The resulting string of digits (numbers greater than 9 becoming two separate digits) are added up. Subtract this sum from the smallest number ending with zero that is greater than or equal to it. This gives the check digit which is also known as the ten's complement of the sum modulo 10.

Profiling

When profiling an ISIN number the first thing to look at is the data type. Is it a Char value? If it is inferred as a VarChar, you then know you have some issues. Since an ISIN is a 12-character value, all ISIN s should be inferred as a Char value.

Next, look at the length of the field. Again, it should be only twelve characters in length. Anything longer or shorter is incorrect. Also, look at patterns, looking for special characters, blanks, etc.

Another way to validate an ISIN number is to calculate the check digit for the number and compare it to the check digit associated with the number in your data. This verifies if you have a valid ISIN number, not necessarily correct for this instrument. Another way to validate an ISIN is to check first two characters for valid county code. I recommend stripping this off and validating it against an ISO country code table. Just make sure you add XS as a valid country code.

The best way to validate an ISIN number is to consult a trusted source. You can purchase a list of financial instruments that include the valid ISIN number and a description of the instrument.

STOCK EXCHANGE DAILY OFFICIAL LIST (SEDOL) NUMBER

The SEDOL number is a code used by the London Stock Exchange to identify foreign stocks, especially those that aren't actively traded in the U.S. and don't have a CUSIP number.

Allocating and administering SEDOL codes to the marketplace for over 35 years, the London Stock Exchange (LSE) is the U.K. representative of the Association of National Numbering Agencies (ANNA). Combined with SEDOL codes, the LSE allocates global ISIN codes to all U.K.-listed securities. Through its enhanced SEDOL Masterfile service, the LSE provides customers with comprehensive reference data and corporate actions solutions.

SEDOLs consist of two parts: a 6-place alphanumeric code and a trailing check digit. SEDOLs issued prior to January 26, 2004 were comprised only of numbers. For those older SEDOLs, those from Asia typically begin with the numeral 6, and those from the UK typically begin with 0.

Because older SEDOLs may begin with a leading zero, when importing a raw file containing SEDOLs into Excel, care must be taken to import that SEDOL column as text, so that the leading zeros are not dropped.

The check digit for SEDOL uses a weighted sum of the first six digits. Letters are converted to numbers by adding their ordinal position in the alphabet to 9, such that A = 10 and Z = 35. The resulting string of numbers is then multiplied by the weighting factor as follows:

First   1
Second   3
Third   1
Fourth   7
Fifth   3
Sixth   9

The character values are multiplied by the weights. The check digit is modulo 10 (10 – this sum modulo 10).

For British and Irish securities, SEDOLs are converted to ISINs by padding the front with two zeros, then adding the country code on the front and the ISIN check digit at the end. Here is an example:

BAE Systems: 0263494

Profiling

When profiling an SEDOL number the first thing to look at is the data type. Is it a Char value? If it is inferred as a VarChar, then you know you have some issues. Since a SEDOL is a seven-character value, all SEDOLs should be inferred as a CHAR value. Since older SEDOLs (prior to 2004) are all numeric, expect a large portion of the field to be inferred as a number.

Next, look at the length of the field. Again, it should only be seven positions in length. Anything longer or shorter is incorrect. Also, look at patterns, paying attention to special characters, blanks, etc. If I were dealing with data from England, I might want to compare the SEDOL to the ISN. For British and Irish securities, SEDOLs are converted to ISINs by padding the front with two zeros, then adding the country code on the front and the ISIN check digit at the end. If I have both a SEDOL and ISIN for a security, I would try to do cross column validation.

Another way to validate a SEDOL number is to calculate the check digit for the number and compare it to the check digit associated with the number in your data. This verifies if you have a valid SEDOL number, not necessarily correct for this instrument.

The best way to validate an SEDOL number is to consult a trusted source. You can purchase a list of financial instruments that includes the valid SEDOL number and a description of the instrument.

Universal Product Code (UPC)

First, the term "UPC" has been replaced; the new term is UCC-12. The term "UCC" stands for Uniform Commercial Code. The UPC encodes twelve decimal digits as SLLLLLLMRRRRRRE, where S (start) and E (end) are the bit pattern 101, M (middle) is the bit pattern 01010 (called guard bars), and each L (left) and R (right) are digits, each one represented by a 7-bit code. This is a total of 95 bits. To enhance reliability in scanning, the bit pattern for each numeral is designed to be as unique as possible and to feature no more than four 1s or 0s in order.

The UPC contains numerals only, with no letters or other characters. The first L digit is the UPC prefix. The last digit R is a check digit, so that errors in scanning or manual entry can be detected.

UPC Prefixes

UPC prefixes are 0, 1, 6, 7, 8, or 9 for most products

- The numeral 2 is reserved for local use (e.g., in a store or warehouse), for items sold by variable weight. Variable-weight items, such as meats and fresh fruits and vegetables, are assigned a UPC by the store if they are packaged on site. In this case, the LLLLL is the item number, and the _RRRR is either the weight or the price, with the first R determining which.
- The numeral 3 is for drugs by national drug code number. Pharmaceuticals in the U.S. use a national drug code (NDC) number as the remainder of the UPC. Although only over-the-counter drugs are typically scanned at point-of-sale, NDC-based UPCs are used on prescription drug packages as well for inventory purposes.
- The numeral 4 is reserved for local use (e.g., in a store or warehouse), often for loyalty cards.
- The numeral 5 is for coupons, though many stores ignore this and use others. In coupons, the LLLLL represents the coupon code, _RRRR is the coupon's discount amount, and whether that amount is a percent or a literal amount is encoded in the first R.

Variable-length UCC company prefixes are issued with some new UCC-12 identification numbers. Based on a new member's need for capacity to identify their trade items, the UCC will vary the length of the UCC company prefix from six to eleven positions, depending on the trade item numbering requirements of new UCC members. Introducing variable-length prefixes will not impact current members who already have and use their UCC company prefixes. The numbers and symbols they have created or will create using their currently assigned UCC company prefix will continue to be unique everywhere in the world.

By prefixing these with a 0, they become EAN-13 rather than UPC-A. This does not change the check digit. All point-of-sale systems can now scan and read both codes alike.

Check Digit Calculation

In the UPC-A system, the check digit is calculated as follows:

- Add the digits in the odd-numbered positions (e.g., first, third, fifth, etc.) together and multiply by three.
- Add the digits in the even-numbered positions (e.g., second, fourth, sixth, etc.) to the result.
- Subtract the result modulo 10 from ten. The answer modulo 10 is the check digit.

Let's look at an example. This UPC is for a box of tissues. The UPC-A barcode is "03600029145X." Where X is the check digit, X can be calculated by adding the odd-numbered digits (0+6+0+2+1+5 = 14), multiplying by three (14 × 3 = 42), adding the even-numbered digits (42+3+0+0+9+4 = 58), calculating modulo 10 (58%10 = 8), subtracting from ten (10 - 8 = 2) and making modulo 10 (2%10 = 2). The check digit is thus 2.

Profiling

When profiling UPC data, the first thing to look at is the data type. Since the UPC can be only numbers, the inferred data type should be a number. The length should be twelve or thirteen digits. Patterns should be of little use since you should only see 9(12) or 9(13). Anything else should be an error.

As with the financial instruments, you can always calculate the check digit and compare it to the check digit that is in the UPC. You can also validate the first digit, which should be 0, 1, 6, 7, 8, or 9 for most products.

The best way to validate the UPC is be to compare it against a valid value table. Nulls are always a question; should a UPC field ever be null or blank? Also, UPC fields should be unique in a reference table, but they should not be in an order or transaction file.

Census Region

When dealing with census data, it is good to know how the U.S. Census Bureau divides the country into regions. This method of division could be used to validate the state against the region. Here are the census regions and the states contained in each:

Northeast

New England: Connecticut, Maine, Massachusetts, New Hampshire, Vermont, and Rhode Island
Middle Atlantic: New Jersey, New York, and Pennsylvania

Midwest

East North Central: Illinois, Indiana, Michigan, Ohio, and Wisconsin
West North Central: Iowa, Kansas, Minnesota, Missouri, Nebraska, North Dakota, and South Dakota

South

South Atlantic: Delaware, District of Columbia, Florida, Georgia, Maryland, North Carolina, South Carolina, Virginia, and West Virginia

East South Central: Alabama, Kentucky, Mississippi, and Tennessee

West

South Central: Arkansas, Louisiana, Oklahoma, and Texas
West Mountain: Arizona, Colorado, Idaho, Montana, Nevada,
New Mexico, Utah, and Wyoming
Pacific: Alaska, California, Hawaii, Oregon, and Washington

FEDEX TRACKING NUMBER

Over the years, FedEx has moved from using 9-digit to 10-digit to the current 12-digit tracking numbers. Old shipping forms are still in circulation, however, and you fill one of these out and drop it off, FedEx still accepts your package. Therefore, you see FedEx tracking numbers using nine, ten, or twelve digits.

To profile FedEx tracking numbers, the first thing to look at is the data type. Has it been inferred as a number? Anything else is an error and, therefore, the field contains invalid tracking numbers. Look at patterns to make sure they conform to the following:

9(12)
9(10)
9(9)

Unless you work for FedEx, or your company tracks each time a package is touched (like FedEx), you should have unique tracking numbers. And if you are keeping track of packages using the FedEx tracking number, should you ever allow nulls in the data?

Drug Enforcement Agency (DEA) Number

A DEA number is a series of letters and numbers assigned to a health care provider (such as a physician, nurse practitioner, or physician's assistant), which grants the provider permission to write prescriptions for controlled substances. Legally, the DEA number is solely used for tracking controlled substances. However, the health care industry often uses the DEA number as a general prescriber number that is a unique identifier for anyone prescribing medication.

A valid DEA number consists of:

Two letters and seven digits
The first letter is either an A or a B
The second letter is the initial of the registrant's last name

The seventh digit is a checksum that is calculated as:

Add together the first, third, and fifth digits
Add together the second, fourth, and sixth digits and
multiply the sum by 2 Add the above two numbers The
last digit (the one's value) of this last sum is used as the
seventh digit in the DEA number

Due to the large type A (practitioner) registrant population, the initial alpha letter B has been exhausted. DEA will begin using the new alpha letter F as the initial character for all new registration for type A (practitioner) registrations.

DEA assigns a unique identification number (UIN) to office-based opioid treatment (OBOT) practitioners. If a practitioner is approved by the Center for Substance Abuse Treatment (CSAT) to conduct office-based opioid treatment, a unique identification number is printed on the practitioner's registration certificate along with the DEA number. The DEA registration number and UIN appear on the printed certificate as such:

AB0123454
XB0123454

The UIN is the same as the DEA registration number, with an X substituted for the first character of the DEA registration number. If an National Technical Information Service (NTIS) user wants to verify a practitioner's UIN, the user must first look up the registrant by DEA registration number and then verify that the practitioner has a business activity code C and a business activity sub code 1. Additional business activity and sub codes are detailed in Table 6.11.

Business Activity	Sub code	Description
A	0	Retail Pharmacy
A	1	Central Fill Pharmacy
A	3	Chain Pharmacy
A	4	Automated Dispensing System
B	0	Hospital/Clinic
C	0	Practitioner
C	1	Practitioner-Dw/30
C	2	Practitioner-Military
C	3	Mlp-Military
C	4	Practitioner-Dw/100
D	0	Teaching Institution
E	0	Manufacturer

E	1	Manufacturer (C I,Ii Bulk)
F	0	Distributor
G	0	Researcher
G	1	Canine Handler
H	0	Analytical Lab
J	0	Importer
J	1	Importer (C I,Ii)
K	0	Exporter
L	0	Reverse Distributor
M	1	Mlp-Ambulance Service
M	2	Mlp-Animal Shelter
M	3	Mlp-Dr Of Oriental Medicine
M	4	Mlp-Dept Of State
M	5	Mlp-Euthanasia Technician
M	6	Mlp-Homeopathic Physician
M	7	Mlp-Medical Psychologist
M	8	Mlp-Naturopathic Physician
M	9	Mlp-Nursing Home

M	A	Mlp-Nurse Practioner
M	B	Mlp-Optometrist
M	C	Mlp-Physician Assistant
M	D	Mlp-Registered Pharmacist
N	0	Maintenance
P	0	Detoxification
R	0	Maintenance & Detox
S	0	Compounder/ Maintenance
T	0	Compounder/ Detoxification
U	0	Compounder/Maint & Detox

Table 6.11

Profiling

To profile DEA numbers, start by looking at the data type. Is it a Char 9? Anything else is invalid. The same thing is true when looking at patterns. Just because it was inferred as a Char 9 does not mean it might have alpha characters in the last seven positions. Expect to see a patter of UU(9)7. Other patterns would be invalid.

A rule would look at the first character of the last name and compare it to the second character of the DEA number. This should not be a hard and fast rule because pharmacies and hospitals are also issued a DEA number. Therefore, the rule needs to be modified to determine if the DEA number has been issued to an institution or an individual. You could calculate the check digit and compare it to the last digit of the DEA number. You could also look for a trusted source of all valid and active DEA numbers.

Uniqueness may also be an issue. Are you tracking transactions that include the DEA number? Are you looking at a reference table of practitioners (e.g., your customers, employees, etc?) Does the number of distinct values look appropriate?

NATIONAL DRUG CODE (NDC) NUMBER

Each listed drug product is assigned a unique 10-digit, three-segment number. This number, known as the NDC, identifies the labeler, product, and trade package size.

The first segment – the labeler code – is assigned by the FDA. A labeler is any firm that manufactures (including repackers or relabelers), or distributes the drug under its own name.

The second segment – the product code – identifies a specific strength, dosage form, and formulation for a particular firm.

The third segment – the package code – identifies package sizes and types. Both the product and package codes are assigned by the firm. The NDC will be in one of the following configurations: 4-4-2, 5-3-2, or 5-4-1.

An asterisk may appear in either a product code or a package code. It simply acts as a placeholder and indicates the configuration of the NDC. Since the NDC is limited to ten digits, a firm with a five- digit labeler code must choose between a three-digit product code and two-digit package code, or a four-digit product code and one-digit package code.

Thus, you have either a 5-4-1 or a 5-3-2 configuration for the three segments of the NDC. Because of a conflict with the HIPAA standard of an 11-digit NDC, many programs will pad the product code or package code segments of the NDC with a leading zero instead of the asterisk.

Since a zero can be a valid digit in the NDC, confusion may result when trying to reconstitute the NDC back to its FDA standard. Here's an example: 12345-0678-09 (eleven digits) may be

12345-678-09 or 12345-0678-9 depending on the firm's configuration. By storing the segments as character data and using the * as placeholders, the confusion is eliminated. In the example, FDA stores the segments as 12345-*678-09 for a 5-3-2 configuration or 12345-0678-*9 for a 5-4-1 configuration.

Profiling

When profiling NDC number data, look at the data type first. Is it inferred as a character or a number? You are looking to see if an asterisk is included or if there are separators. When I worked with NDC data, it was stored by the company as a number. My customer was not concerned about looking at the segments. In addition, because of the different configurations, it is difficult to profile NDC number data field without some way of segmenting the different parts. Just looking at the field as a whole gives you no indication on how to break it out. Also, is it the 10- or 11-character version of the number? Pattern analysis helps sort many of these issues.

The best thing to do is find a trusted source and validate the data against this source.

NATIONAL PROVIDER IDENTIFIER (NPI)

For over 25 years, the National Council for Prescription Drug Programs (NCPDP) has assigned a unique number to pharmacies in the United States and its territories. All pharmacies must obtain an NPI. This number identifies pharmacies to health plan claims processors and third-party contractors. The information the NCPDP maintains about pharmacies is also used in the following ways:

- To help electronic prescribing vendors identify a pharmacy
- To help patients locate the nearest pharmacy via the Web

- To help mailing organizations notify patients of important drug recalls.

The NPI is an eight-position alphanumeric identifier. It includes as the eighth position a numeric check digit to assist in identifying erroneous or invalid NPIs. The check digit algorithm must be computed from an all-numeric base number. Therefore, any alpha characters that may be part of the NPI are translated to specific numerics before the calculation of the check digit. The NPI format allows for the creation of approximately 20 billion unique identifiers.

The eight-position alphanumeric format was chosen over a longer numeric-only format to keep the identifier as short as possible while providing for an identifier pool that serves the industry's longer term needs. The NCPDA will issue numeric-only identifiers first and introduce alphabetic characters starting with the first position of the NPI. Doing so affords health care providers and health plans additional time to accommodate the alphabetic characters.

DATA UNIVERSAL NUMBERING SYSTEM (DUNS) NUMBER

The Data Universal Numbering System, abbreviated as DUNS or D-U-N-S, is a system developed and regulated by Dun & Bradstreet (D&B), which assigns a unique numeric identifier to a single business entity. This numeric identifier is then referred to as a DUNS number. It was introduced in 1963 to support D&B's credit reporting practice. The system has gained wide acceptance globally and is a common standard. Its users include the European Commission, the United Nations, and the United States government. It is recognized, recommended, and/or required by more than 50 global, industry, and trade associations. The DUNS database has over 57 million entries for business throughout the world, according to the Federal Procurement Data Center's DUNS search page.

The DUNS number is a nine-digit number assigned to each business in the D&B database that has a unique, separate, and distinct operation. There is no charge to obtain a DUNS number, which takes about 30 days to be issued. The number is issued at random, and the digits apparently have no significance as to their issuance. According to the D&B Web site, each DUNS number contains a mod 10 check digit to support error detection.

A DUNS number is sometimes formatted with embedded dashes to promote readability, such as 15-048-3782. Modern usage typically omits dashes and shows the number in the form 150483782 (this is the actual DUNS number of Dun & Bradstreet).

Unlike the employer identification number (EIN) issued by the Internal Revenue Service, a DUNS number may be issued to any business worldwide. Certain federal government agencies require their vendors to have a DUNS number as well as an EIN. Other agencies, such as some United Nations offices and Australian government agencies, require certain businesses to have a D-U-N-S number. DUNS numbers are now also issued to individuals; previously, DUNS numbers could only be obtained by corporations or other organizations.

Numerous other business-numbering systems exist independent of DUNS—for example the International Suppliers Network system. However, few, if any, have the volume of international businesses that are registered by DUNS.

In the June 27, 2003 issue of the Federal Register (68 FR 38402), the U.S. Office of Management and Budget (OMB) announced that a DUNS number is required for all grant applicants for new or renewal awards on or after October 1, 2003. The DUNS number supplements other identifiers (e.g., EIN) and is required whether an applicant is using paper or electronic application processes.

The DUNS number replaced another coding system known as the Architect-Engineer Contract Administration Support System (ACASS). The ACASS number was abolished when the ACASS system transitioned to a modernized platform on October 5, 2005.

The ACASS system now uses the DUNS number in place of an ACASS number. Firms should supply their DUNS number, and notify the requestor of the discontinuation of the ACASS number, when asked for their ACASS number.

Chapter 7

SUMMARY

NOW you know the many different techniques for profiling data. I hope that most of them are new to you. While you do not need an automated data profiling tool to do this work, I hope you consider buying a tool. This can significantly reduce your risk of a data integration or data quality project.

Despite careful initial planning, four out of five (83 percent) of data migration projects over $1 million are at risk of overrunning in time and cost, or of outright failure, according to The Standish Group report "Migrate Headaches."

According to The Standish Group report, one of the primary causes of data migration project overruns and failures is a lack of understanding of the source data prior to data movement. This study involved a series of focus groups with IT executives in four U.S. cities. According to these executives, 60–80 percent of the effort in data migration projects is expended on trying to understand and map the source data. They also indicated that this was an iterative process without a predictable endpoint. The study concluded that if source data could be understood more efficiently and accurately, then the project's business value could be delivered on time, or even accelerated.

Understanding data can be hard work. Why? Reasons include:

- Manual data profiling is tedious, slow, labor intensive, and error prone.

- Metadata documentation may be missing, incomplete, or badly out of date.
- Source code for legacy systems may no longer be found.
- Relationships between data elements are not always obvious.
- Databases are not static; over time, they may be corrupted.

But the rewards for understanding data are significant. Data profiling yields high returns on investment by:

- Reducing direct project costs such as labor and resources
- Increasing project value through early project completion
- Reducing unexpected costs and delayed benefits associated with overruns or cancellations
- Increasing the quality of the migrated or converted data without extending deadlines

According to Estelle De Beer, BI practice manager at Sybase SA:

Using manual data profiling, at an employee cost per hour of R110 and five hours/attribute, the cost per attribute is R550. If there are 2500 attributes to be profiled, the total cost is R1 375 000. With automated data profiling, the time taken is reduced to 30 minutes/attribute, so the actual cost is R137 500.

This results in a return on investment, after investing R650 000 in a data profiling tool, of R587 500 for the first project. The ROI for every additional project of the same size is R1 237 500.

A data profiling solution can help companies gain a complete and accurate understanding of source data and minimize risk in projects dependent upon that data.

It can also:

* *Accelerate project completion*

* *Dramatically reduce both expected and unexpected (overrun) project costs*
* *Increase the quality of project results*
* *Help gain a thorough understanding of corporate data quality, content, relationships, and structure prior to engaging in data migration, integration, or consolidation projects.*
* *Correct inconsistencies, redundancies, and inaccuracies in corporate databases - the essential first step in any successful data-driven IT initiative.*

I remember when I was involved with data warehouses. The tools used to build these data warehouses were a function of who was a member of the project team. On one project we used SQL to sample the data. On another, the team included an SAS expert. On yet another project we used Microsoft Access® to take a sample and look at the data.

What happens when your SAS expert goes on vacation? In our case, the profiling came to a screeching halt. But with a business-friendly automated profiling tool that everyone on the team can use, profiling can continue regardless of the vacation status of your technology expert. An automated profiling tool enables your team members to share a common vocabulary and, using a built-in profiling process, collaborate effectively cross-functionally through the project's duration.

Many companies have used automated data profiling tools with much success. Here's what some of them have to say about the ROI gained from these tools:

* "Revealed ROI within 8 months of purchase through labor hours and accuracy."
* "Identified risks and inaccuracies involved with working with source data. Example: >50% reduction on hours for analysis by using an automated data profiling tool"
* "Turnaround time of data analysis requests use to be about two to three weeks. Now it's overnight."

Consider these important benefits when deciding to use a profiling tool. I wish you good profiling and great success as you gain a deeper, more thorough understanding of your data.

APPENDICES

Appendix 1: Valid State Code Table

State /Possession	Abbreviation	State/Possession	Abbreviation
Alabama	AL	Alaska	AK
American Samoa	AS	Arizona	AZ
Arkansas	AR	California	CA
Colorado	CO	Connecticut	CT
Delaware	DE	District Of Columbia	DC
Federated States Of Micronesia	FM	Florida	FL
Georgia	GA	Guam	GU
Hawaii	HI	Idaho	ID
Illinois	IL	Indiana	IN
Iowa	IA	Kansas	KS
Kentucky	KY	Louisiana	LA
Maine	ME	Marshall Islands	MH
Maryland	MD	Massachusetts	MA
Michigan	MI	Minnesota	MN
Mississippi	MS	Missouri	MO
Montana	MT	Nebraska	NE
Nevada	NV	New Hampshire	NH
New Jersey	NJ	New Mexico	NM

New York	NY	North Carolina	NC
North Dakota	ND	Northern Mariana Islands	MP
Ohio	OH	Oklahoma	OK
Oregon	OR	Palau	PW
Pennsylvania	PA	Puerto Rico	PR
Rhode Island	RI	South Carolina	SC
South Dakota	SD	Tennessee	TN
Texas	TX	Utah	UT
Vermont	VT	Virgin Islands	VI
Virginia	VA	Washington	WA
West Virginia	WV	Wisconsin	WI
Wyoming	WY	Armed Forces Africa	AE
Armed Forces Americas(Except Canada)	AA	Armed Forces Canada	AE
Armed Forces Europe	AE	Armed Forces Middle East	AE
Armed Forces Pacific	AP		

Appendix 2: Valid Country Names and Codes

AFGHANISTAN	AF
ÅLAND ISLANDS	AX
ALBANIA	AL
ALGERIA	DZ
AMERICAN SAMOA	AS
ANDORRA	AD
ANGOLA	AO
ANGUILLA	AI
ANTARCTICA	AQ
ANTIGUA AND BARBUDA	AG
ARGENTINA	AR
ARMENIA	AM
ARUBA	AW
AUSTRALIA	AU
AUSTRIA	AT
AZERBAIJAN	AZ
BAHAMAS	BS
BAHRAIN	BH
BANGLADESH	BD
BARBADOS	BB
BELARUS	BY
BELGIUM	BE
BELIZE	BZ
BENIN	BJ
BERMUDA	BM
BHUTAN	BT
BOLIVIA	BO
BOSNIA AND HERZEGOVINA	BA
BOTSWANA	BW
BOUVET ISLAND	BV

BRAZIL	BR
BRITISH INDIAN OCEAN TERRITORY	IO
BRUNEI DARUSSALAM	BN
BULGARIA	BG
BURKINA FASO	BF
BURUNDI	BI
CAMBODIA	KH
CAMEROON	CM
CANADA	CA
CAPE VERDE	CV
CAYMAN ISLANDS	KY
CENTRAL AFRICAN REPUBLIC	CF
CHAD	TD
CHILE	CL
CHINA	CN
CHRISTMAS ISLAND	CX
COCOS (KEELING) ISLANDS	CC
COLOMBIA	CO
COMOROS	KM
CONGO	CG
CONGO, THE DEMOCRATIC REPUBLIC OF THE	CD
COOK ISLANDS	CK
COSTA RICA	CR
CÔTE DíIVOIRE	CI
CROATIA	HR
CUBA	CU
CYPRUS	CY
CZECH REPUBLIC	CZ

DENMARK	DK
DJIBOUTI	DJ
DOMINICA	DM
DOMINICAN REPUBLIC	DO
ECUADOR	EC
EGYPT	EG
EL SALVADOR	SV
EQUATORIAL GUINEA	GQ
ERITREA	ER
ESTONIA	EE
ETHIOPIA	ET
FALKLAND ISLANDS (MALVINAS)	FK
FAROE ISLANDS	FO
FIJI	FJ
FINLAND	FI
FRANCE	FR
FRENCH GUIANA	GF
FRENCH POLYNESIA	PF
FRENCH SOUTHERN TERRITORIES	TF
GABON	GA
GAMBIA	GM
GEORGIA	GE
GERMANY	DE
GHANA	GH
GIBRALTAR	GI
GREECE	GR
GREENLAND	GL
GRENADA	GD
GUADELOUPE	GP
GUAM	GU
GUATEMALA	GT
GUERNSEY	GG

GUINEA	GN
GUINEA-BISSAU	GW
GUYANA	GY
HAITI	HT
HEARD ISLAND AND MCDONALD ISLANDS	HM
HOLY SEE (VATICAN CITY STATE)	VA
HONDURAS	HN
HONG KONG	HK
HUNGARY	HU
ICELAND	IS
INDIA	IN
INDONESIA	ID
IRAN, ISLAMIC REPUBLIC OF	IR
IRAQ	IQ
IRELAND	IE
ISLE OF MAN	IM
ISRAEL	IL
ITALY	IT
JAMAICA	JM
JAPAN	JP
JERSEY	JE
JORDAN	JO
KAZAKHSTAN	KZ
KENYA	KE
KIRIBATI	KI
KOREA, DEMOCRATIC PEOPLE'S REPUBLIC OF	KP
KOREA, REPUBLIC OF	KR
KUWAIT	KW
KYRGYZSTAN	KG
LAO PEOPLE'S DEMOCRATIC REPUBLIC	LA

LATVIA	LV	NAURU	NR
LEBANON	LB	NEPAL	NP
LESOTHO	LS	NETHERLANDS ANTILLES	AN
LIBERIA	LR	NETHERLANDS	NL
LIBYAN ARAB JAMAHIRIYA	LY	NEW CALEDONIA	NC
LIECHTENSTEIN	LI	NEW ZEALAND	NZ
LITHUANIA	LT	NICARAGUA	NI
LUXEMBOURG	LU	NIGER	NE
MACAO	MO	NIGERIA	NG
MACEDONIA, THE FORMER YUGOSLAV REPUBLIC OF	MK	NIUE	NU
		NORFOLK ISLAND	NF
MADAGASCAR	MG	NORTHERN MARIANA ISLANDS	MP
MALAWI	MW		
MALAYSIA	MY	NORWAY	NO
MALDIVES	MV	OMAN	OM
MALI	ML	PAKISTAN	PK
MALTA	MT	PALAU	PW
MARSHALL ISLANDS	MH	PALESTINIAN TERRITORY, OCCUPIED	PS
MARTINIQUE	MQ		
MAURITANIA	MR	PANAMA	PA
MAURITIUS	MU	PAPUA NEW GUINEA	PG
MAYOTTE	YT	PARAGUAY	PY
MEXICO	MX	PERU	PE
MICRONESIA, FEDERATED STATES OF	FM	PHILIPPINES	PH
		PITCAIRN	PN
MOLDOVA, REPUBLIC OF	MD	POLAND	PL
MONACO	MC	PORTUGAL	PT
MONGOLIA	MN	PUERTO RICO	PR
MONTENEGRO	ME	QATAR	QA
MONTSERRAT	MS	RÉUNION	RE
MOROCCO	MA	ROMANIA	RO
MOZAMBIQUE	MZ	RUSSIAN FEDERATION	RU
MYANMAR	MM	RWANDA	RW
NAMIBIA	NA	SAINT HELENA	SH

SAINT KITTS AND NEVIS	KN		TANZANIA, UNITED REPUBLIC OF	TZ
SAINT LUCIA	LC			
SAINT PIERRE AND MIQUELON	PM		THAILAND	TH
			TIMOR-LESTE	TL
SAINT VINCENT AND THE GRENADINES	VC		TOGO	TG
			TOKELAU	TK
SAMOA	WS		TONGA	TO
SAN MARINO	SM		TRINIDAD AND TOBAGO	TT
SAO TOME AND PRINCIPE	ST		TUNISIA	TN
SAUDI ARABIA	SA		TURKEY	TR
SENEGAL	SN		TURKMENISTAN	TM
SERBIA	RS		TURKS AND CAICOS ISLANDS	TC
SEYCHELLES	SC			
SIERRA LEONE	SL		TUVALU	TV
SINGAPORE	SG		UGANDA	UG
SLOVAKIA	SK		UKRAINE	UA
SLOVENIA	SI		UNITED ARAB EMIRATES	AE
SOLOMON ISLANDS	SB		UNITED KINGDOM	GB
SOMALIA	SO		UNITED STATES MINOR OUTLYING ISLANDS	UM
SOUTH AFRICA	ZA			
SOUTH GEORGIA AND THE SOUTH SANDWICH ISLANDS	GS		UNITED STATES	US
			URUGUAY	UY
SPAIN	ES		UZBEKISTAN	UZ
SRI LANKA	LK		VANUATU	VU
SUDAN	SD		VENEZUELA	VE
SURINAME	SR		VIET NAM	VN
SVALBARD AND JAN MAYEN	SJ		VIRGIN ISLANDS, BRITISH	VG
SWAZILAND	SZ		VIRGIN ISLANDS, US	VI
SWEDEN	SE		WALLIS AND FUTUNA	WF
SWITZERLAND	CH		WESTERN SAHARA	EH
SYRIAN ARAB REPUBLIC	SY		YEMEN	YE
TAIWAN, PROVINCE OF CHINA	TW		ZAMBIA	ZM
			ZIMBABWE	ZW
TAJIKISTAN	TJ			

Appendix 3: North American Area Code Table

Area Code	Location
201	NJ
202	DC
203	CT
204	Manitoba
205	AL
206	WA
207	ME
208	ID
209	CA
210	TX
212	NY
213	CA
214	TX
215	PA
216	OH
217	IL
218	MN
219	IN
224	IL
225	LA
228	MS
229	GA
231	MI
234	OH
239	FL
240	MD
242	Bahamas
246	Barbados
248	MI
250	British Columbia
251	AL
252	NC
253	WA

254	TX
256	AL
260	IN
262	WI
264	Anguilla
267	PA
268	Antigua/Barbuda
269	MI
270	KY
276	VA
281	TX
284	British Virgin Islands
289	Ontario
301	MD
302	DE
303	CO
304	WV
305	FL
306	Saskatchewan
307	WY
308	NE
309	IL
310	CA
312	IL
313	MI
314	MO
315	NY
316	KS
317	IN
318	LA
319	IA
320	MN
321	FL
323	CA
325	TX

330	OH		440	OH
334	AL		441	Bermuda
336	NC		443	MD
337	LA		450	Quebec
339	MA		456	NANP area
340	USVI		469	TX
345	Cayman Islands		473	Grenada
347	NY		478	GA
351	MA		479	AR
352	FL		480	AZ
360	WA		484	PA
361	TX		500	NANP area
386	FL		501	AR
401	RI		502	KY
402	NE		503	OR
403	Alberta		504	LA
404	GA		505	NM
405	OK		506	New Brunswick
406	MT		507	MN
407	FL		508	MA
408	CA		509	WA
409	TX		510	CA
410	MD		512	TX
412	PA		513	OH
413	MA		514	Quebec
414	WI		515	IA
415	CA		516	NY
416	Ontario		517	MI
417	MO		518	NY
418	Quebec		519	Ontario
419	OH		520	AZ
423	TN		530	CA
424	CA		540	VA
425	WA		541	OR
430	TX		551	NJ
432	TX		559	CA
434	VA		561	FL
435	UT		562	CA

563	IA
567	OH
570	PA
571	VA
573	MO
574	IN
580	OK
585	NY
586	MI
600	Canada
601	MS
602	AZ
603	NH
604	British Columbia
605	SD
606	KY
607	NY
608	WI
609	NJ
610	PA
612	MN
613	Ontario
614	OH
615	TN
616	MI
617	MA
618	IL
619	CA
620	KS
623	AZ
626	CA
630	IL
631	NY
636	MO
641	IA
646	NY
647	Ontario
649	Turks & Caicos Islands

650	CA
651	MN
660	MO
661	CA
662	MS
664	Montserrat
670	CNMI
671	GU
678	GA
682	TX
684	AS
700	NANP area
701	ND
702	NV
703	VA
704	NC
705	Ontario
706	GA
707	CA
708	IL
709	Newfoundland
710	US
712	IA
713	TX
714	CA
715	WI
716	NY
717	PA
718	NY
719	CO
720	CO
724	PA
727	FL
731	TN
732	NJ
734	MI
740	OH
754	FL
757	VA

758	St. Lucia		829	Dominican Republic
760	CA		830	TX
763	MN		831	CA
765	IN		832	TX
767	Dominica		843	SC
769	MS		845	NY
770	GA		847	IL
772	FL		848	NJ
773	IL		850	FL
774	MA		856	NJ
775	NV		857	MA
778	British Columbia		858	CA
780	Alberta		859	KY
781	MA		860	CT
784	St. Vincent & Grenadines		862	NJ
			863	FL
785	KS		864	SC
786	FL		865	TN
787	Puerto Rico		866	NANP area
800	NANP area		867	Yukon
801	UT		868	Trinidad & Tobago
802	VT		869	St. Kitts & Nevis
803	SC		870	AR
804	VA		876	Jamaica
805	CA		877	NANP area
806	TX		878	PA
807	Ontario		888	NANP area
808	HI		900	NANP area
809	Dominican Republic		901	TN
810	MI		902	Nova Scotia
812	IN		903	TX
813	FL		904	FL
814	PA		905	Ontario
815	IL		906	MI
816	MO		907	AK
817	TX		908	NJ
818	CA		909	CA
819	Quebec		910	NC
828	NC		912	GA

913	KS
914	NY
915	TX
916	CA
917	NY
918	OK
919	NC
920	WI
925	CA
928	AZ
931	TN
936	TX
937	OH
939	Puerto Rico
940	TX
941	FL
947	MI
949	CA
951	CA
952	MN
954	FL
956	TX
970	CO
971	OR
972	TX
973	NJ
978	MA
979	TX
980	NC
985	LA
989	MI

Appendix 4: Non-Geographic Area Codes In Service

456	Inbound International
500	Personal Communication Service
600	Canadian Services
700	Interexchange Carrier Services
710	US Government
800	Toll-Free
866	Toll-Free
877	Toll-Free
888	Toll-Free
900	Premium Services

Appendix 5: Planned Area Codes New NPA

NPA	State or Provence
226	Ontario
227	MD
283	OH
331	IL
341	CA
369	CA
380	OH
385	UT
438	Quebec
442	CA
447	IL
464	IL
470	GA
475	CT
557	MO
959	CT
975	MO

564	WA
627	CA
628	CA
657	CA
659	AL
667	MD
669	CA
679	MI
689	FL
730	IL
737	TX
747	CA
762	GA
764	CA
779	IL
872	IL
935	CA
984	NC

Appendix 6 : Driver's License Guidelines

The following is a list of states and the required format for driver's licenses.

ALABAMA (AL)
Format: 7 Numeric

ALASKA (AK)
Format: 1–7 Numeric

ARIZONA (AZ)
Format 1 Alphabetic, 8 Numeric; or 2 Alphabetic, 3–6 Numeric; or 9 Numeric (SSN); or 9 Numeric.

ARKANSAS (AR)
Format: 9 Numeric (SSN), if not SSN, will start with 9
If 9 digit (SSN), must include Date of Birth. SSN should only be used if it appears on the license.

CALIFORNIA (CA)
Format: 1 Alphabetic, 7 Numeric

COLORADO (CO)
Format: 9 Numeric
State issuing 9 numeric format for all renewals since 1994

CONNECTICUT (CT)
Format: 9 Numeric, first two positions are month of birth in odd or even year. 01–12 Jan–Dec odd years, 13–24 Jan–Dec even years, 99 unknown

DELAWARE (DE)
Format: 1–7 Numeric

DISTRICT OF COLUMBIA (DC)
Format: 9 Numeric (SSN) or 7 Numeric

FLORIDA (FL)
Format: 1 Alphabetic, 12 Numeric

GEORGIA (GA)
Format: 7–9 Numeric or SSN

HAWAII (HI)
Format: 9 Numeric or "H" + 8 numeric

IDAHO (ID)
Format: 2 Alphabetic, 6 Numeric, 1 Alphabetic; or 9 Numeric (SSN); or 9 Numeric

ILLINOIS (IL)
Format: 1 Alphabetic, 11 Numeric

INDIANA (IN)
Format: 10 Numeric or 9 Numeric (SSN)

IOWA (IA)
Format: 9 Numeric (SSN); or 3 Numeric, 2 Alphabetic, 4 Numeric

KANSAS (KS)
Format: 9 Numeric (SSN); or 1 Alphabetic (K), 8 Numeric

KENTUCKY (KY)
Format: 9 Numeric (SSN); or 1 Alphabetic, 8 Numeric

LOUISIANA (LA)
Format: 9 Numeric, first 2 numbers are always zeros, then 7 Numeric

MAINE (ME)
Format: 7 Numeric or if under 21, 7 Numeric followed by an "X"

MARYLAND (MD)
Format: 1 Alphabetic, 12 Numeric

MASSACHUSETTS (MA)
Format: 1 Alphabetic, 8 Numeric; or 9 Numeric (SSN)

MICHIGAN (MI)
Format: 1 Alphabetic, 12 Numeric

MINNESOTA (MN)
Format: 1 Alphabetic, 12 Numeric

MISSISSIPPI (MS)
Format: 9 Numeric (usually SSN)

MISSOURI (MO)
Format: 1 Alphabetic, 5–9 Numeric or 9 Numeric; or 9 Numeric (SSN)

MONTANA (MT)
Format: 9 Numeric (SSN); or 1 Alphabetic, 1 Numeric, 1 Alpha numeric, 2 Numeric, 3 Alphabetic and 1 Numeric; or 13 Numeric

NEBRASKA (NE)
Format: 1 Alphabetic (A, B, C, E, G, H, or V), 3–8 Numeric

NEVADA (NV)
Format: 12 Numeric (last 2 are year of birth), or 10 numeric

NEW HAMPSHIRE (NH)
Format: 2 Numeric, 3 Alphabetic, 5 Numeric

NEW JERSEY (NJ)
Format: 1 Alphabetic, 14 Numeric

NEW MEXICO (NM)
Format: 9 Numeric

NEW YORK (NY)
Format: 9 Numeric (not SSN); or 1 Alphabetic, 18 Numeric

NORTH CAROLINA (NC)
Format: 1–8 Numeric

NORTH DAKOTA (ND)
Format: 9 Numeric (SSN) or 9 Numeric for non-CDL beginning with #9 or 3 alphabetic, 6 numeric

OHIO (OH)
Format: 9 Numeric (SSN); or 2 Alphabetic, 6 Numeric *Always use the SSN as DL #, if available!*

OKLAHOMA (OK)
Format: 9 Numeric or 1 alpha/numeric, 9 numeric

OREGON (OR)
Format: 1–7 Numeric

PENNSYLVANIA (PA)
Format: 8 Numeric

RHODE ISLAND (RI)
Format: 7 Numeric or V and 6 Numeric (disabled veterans)

SOUTH CAROLINA (SC)
Format: 6 to 9 Numeric

SOUTH DAKOTA (SD)
Format: 8 Numeric, or 9 Numeric (SSN)

TENNESSEE (TN)
Format: 7 to 9 Numeric

TEXAS (TX)
Format: 8 Numeric beginning with 0, 1, or 2

UTAH (UT)
Format: 4–10 Numeric

VERMONT (VT)
Format: 8 Numeric; or 7 Numeric, letter A

VIRGINIA (VA)
Format: 9 Numeric (SSN); or 1 Alphabetic, 8 Numeric

WASHINGTON (WA)
Format: 5 Alphabetic (last name), 1 Alphabetic (first name), 1 Alphabetic (middle name), 3 Numeric, 2 Alphanumeric *If last or middle name field falls short, please fill with *'s*

WEST VIRGINIA (WV)
Format: 1 Alpha must be either zero or A, B, C, D, E, F, S and 6 Numeric;

or must be 1X and 5 Numeric; or letters XX and 5 Numeric

WISCONSIN (WI)
Format: 1 Alphabetic, 13 Numeric

WYOMING (WY)
Format: 10 Numeric or 9 Numeric (i.e., 123456-123)

Appendix 7: American Petroleum Institute State Code Table

State	Code
Alabama	1
Arizona	2
Arkansas	3
California	4
Colorado	5
Connecticut	6
Delaware	7
District of Columbia	8
Florida	9
Georgia	10
Idaho	11
Illinois	12
Indiana	13
Iowa	14
Kansas	15
Kentucky	16
Louisiana	17
Maine	18
Maryland	19
Massachusetts	20
Michigan	21
Minnesota	22
Mississippi	23
Missouri	24
Montana	25
Nebraska	26
Nevada	27
New Hampshire	28
New Jersey	29

State	Code
New Mexico	30
New York	31
North Carolina	32
North Dakota	33
Ohio	34
Oklahoma	35
Oregon	36
Pennsylvania	37
Rhode Island	38
South Carolina	39
South Dakota	40
Tennessee	41
Texas	42
Utah	43
Vermont	44
Virginia	45
Washington	46
West Virginia	47
Wisconsin	48
Wyoming	49
Alaska	50
Hawaii	51
Alaska Offshore	55
Pacific Coast Offshore	56
Northern Gulf of Mexico	60
Atlantic Coast Offshore	61

Bibliography

Larry P. English: *Improving Data Warehouse and Business Information Quality,* John Wiley & Sons Inc., 1999.

Paul Krill: "CRM plagued by data quality issues," INFO-WORLD, Octber 5, 2001

David Loshin: *Enterprise Knowledge Management: The Data Quality Approach,* Morgan Kaufmann, 2001

Jack Olson: *Data Profiling: The Accuracy Dimension,* Morgan Kaufmann, 2002.

PricewaterhouseCoopers, "Global Data Management Survey," 2001.

Thomas C. Redman: *Data Quality for the Information Age,* Artech House, 1996.

Philip Russom: *Taking Data Quality to the Enterprise Through Data Governance,* 2006.

About the Author

ED Lindsey has a BBA in math and information technology and an MBA in Management from Pace University. His career in information technology spans more than 30 years. He has worked on mainframes, mini-computers, and PCs and has done extensive work in voice and data networks. He has certifications with both Microsoft and Cisco. His more recent accomplishments include designing high availability transaction processing systems while working at AT&T Bell Laboratories. He moved from the Labs to NCR Teradata where he was involved with building data warehouses for the communication industry. The data warehouse experience showed him the need for improving data quality. He became involved with data quality in 1999, becoming a trailblazer and preaching the need to profile data. While working at companies like Evoke, Ascential, IBM, Similarity Systems, and now Informatica and working with products like DataFlux dfPower® Studio, Ed has a wealth of experience working with a variety of companies, helping them to identify and fix data quality issue